Editor
Nancy Hoffman

Managing Editor
Karen J. Goldfluss, M.S. Ed.

Cover Artist
Brenda DiAntonis

Art Production Manager
Kevin Barnes

Art Coordinator
Renée Christine Yates

Imaging
Rosa C. See
Ricardo Martinez
James Edward Grace

Publisher
Mary D. Smith, M.S. Ed

Spotlight On
AMERICA

Grades 5 & Up

Westward Movement

Author

Robert W. Smith

Teacher Created Resources, Inc.
6421 Industry Way
Westminster, CA 92683
www.teachercreated.com
ISBN: 978-1-4206-3216-3
©2006 *Teacher Created Resources, Inc.*
Reprinted, 2012
Made in U.S.A.

Table of Contents

Introduction

The Spotlight on America series is designed to introduce significant events in American history to students in the fifth through eighth grades. Reading in the content area is enriched with a balanced variety of activities in written language, literature, social studies, art, science, math, and oral expression. The series is designed to make history literally come alive in your classroom and take root in the minds of your students.

The westward movement of the American people was one of the greatest and most unusual migrations in human history because it was based on individuals and families choosing to relocate instead of being forced to by war or political factions. This century-long migration also expanded the boundaries of the United States from the Atlantic Ocean to the Pacific Ocean and populated vast stretches of relatively uninhabited land. The American migration created a nation that became first an agricultural power and then an industrial giant.

The frontier allowed poor Americans and immigrants from other countries to own their own homes and farm their own land, creating a fertile climate for the growth and development of democratic government. The westward movement spurred the development of transportation, inventions, communication, industry, and finance. This relentless advance of people across the continent lifted a small, weak, rural nation to the ranks of an international power in one century. The advantages of wealth and land ownership to the American people, however, were offset by the appalling mistreatment of the Native Americans who had lived here for thousands of years as well as the scars imposed on the land and the environment.

The reading selections and comprehension questions in this book introduce the westward movement and set the stage for activities in other subject areas. The literature and language activities are designed to help students understand the feelings, hopes, and dreams of those who uprooted their lives to become pioneers, miners, fur trappers, and frontiersmen. Students should acquire a basic understanding of the major events that led to the transformation of the nation.

The research activities are intended to bring students into the lives of people as diverse as Theodore Roosevelt and Sarah Winnemucca, Jedediah Smith and Sitting Bull, Narcissa Whitman and Sam Houston. The culminating activities are aimed at acquainting students with the life and times of pioneer people.

Enjoy using this book with your students. Look for other books in this series.

Teacher Lesson Plans for Reading Comprehension

The Westward Movement

Objective: Students will demonstrate fluency and comprehension in reading historically-based text.

Materials: copies of The Westward Movement (pages 8 and 9); copies of The Westward Movement Quiz (page 34); additional reading selections from books, encyclopedias, and Internet sources for enrichment

Procedure

1. Reproduce and distribute The Westward Movement. Review pre-reading skills by briefly reviewing the text and encouraging students to underline, make notes in the margins, write questions, and highlight unfamiliar words as they read.

2. Have students read the article independently, in small groups, or together as a class.

3. As a class, discuss the following questions or others of your choosing:
   - Why do you think Americans felt they had a "Manifest Destiny" to settle the continent?
   - Should Americans be proud of their pioneer heritage? Why or why not?
   - How would you have felt if you were a pioneer during the westward movement?

Assessment: Have students complete The Westward Movement Quiz. Correct the quiz together.

Mountain Men

Objective: Students will demonstrate fluency and comprehension in reading historically-based text.

Materials: copies of Mountain Men (pages 10–13); copies of the Mountain Men Quiz (page 35); additional reading selections from books, encyclopedias, and Internet sources for enrichment

Procedure

1. Reproduce and distribute Mountain Men. Review pre-reading skills by briefly reviewing the text and encouraging students to underline, make notes in the margins, write questions, and highlight unfamiliar words as they read.

2. Have students read the article independently, in small groups, or together as a class.

3. As a class, discuss the following questions or others of your choosing:
   - Would you like to have been a mountain man? Give your reasons.
   - Who was the most interesting mountain man? Why?
   - What lifestyles today might be similar to that of the mountain men?

Assessment: Have students complete the Mountain Men Quiz. Correct the quiz together.

Teacher Lesson Plans for Reading Comprehension *(cont.)*

Trails West

Objective: Students will demonstrate fluency and comprehension in reading historically-based text.

Materials: copies of Trails West (pages 14–16); copies of Trails West Quiz (page 36); additional reading selections from books, encyclopedias, and Internet sources for enrichment

Procedure

1. Reproduce and distribute Trails West. Review pre-reading skills by briefly reviewing the text and encouraging students to underline, make notes in the margins, write questions, and highlight unfamiliar words as they read.

2. Have students read the article independently, in small groups, or together as a class.

3. As a class, discuss the following questions or others of your choosing:

   • Which trail would you have taken on the journey west? Why?

   • Which trail do you think was most dangerous? Why?

Assessment: Have students complete the Trails West Quiz. Correct the quiz together.

On the Oregon Trail

Objective: Students will demonstrate fluency and comprehension in reading historically-based text.

Materials: copies of On the Oregon Trail (pages 17–20); copies of On the Oregon Trail Quiz (page 37); additional reading selections from books, encyclopedias, and Internet sources for enrichment

Procedure

1. Reproduce and distribute On the Oregon Trail. Review pre-reading skills by briefly reviewing the text and encouraging students to underline, make notes in the margins, write questions, and highlight unfamiliar words as they read.

2. Have students read the article independently, in small groups, or together as a class.

3. As a class, discuss the following questions or others of your choosing:

   • Why did pioneers get "Oregon Fever"?

   • Would you like to have been a pioneer on the Oregon Trail? Explain your reasons.

   • Were the pioneers along the Oregon Trail heroes? Why or why not?

Assessment: Have students complete the On the Oregon Trail Quiz. Correct the quiz together.

Teacher Lesson Plans for Reading Comprehension *(cont.)*

Pioneer Life

Objective: Students will demonstrate fluency and comprehension in reading historically-based text.

Materials: copies of Pioneer Life (pages 21–24); copies of Pioneer Life Quiz (page 38); additional reading selections from books, encyclopedias, and Internet sources for enrichment

Procedure

1. Reproduce and distribute Pioneer Life. Review pre-reading skills by briefly reviewing the text and encouraging students to underline, make notes in the margins, write questions, and highlight unfamiliar words as they read.

2. Have students read the article independently, in small groups, or together as a class.

3. As a class, discuss the following questions or others of your choosing:

   - Would you like to have been a child growing up in pioneer times? Why or why not?

   - What would have been the best thing about being a pioneer?

   - What would have been the worst thing about being a pioneer?

Assessment: Have students complete the Pioneer Life Quiz. Correct the quiz together.

Striking It Rich

Objective: Students will demonstrate fluency and comprehension in reading historically-based text.

Materials: copies of Striking It Rich (pages 25–27); copies of Striking It Rich Quiz (page 39); additional reading selections from books, encyclopedias, and Internet sources for enrichment

Procedure

1. Reproduce and distribute Striking It Rich. Review pre-reading skills by briefly reviewing the text and encouraging students to underline, make notes in the margins, write questions, and highlight unfamiliar words as they read.

2. Have students read the article independently, in small groups, or together as a class.

3. Talk about these discussion questions or others of your choosing with the students:

   - Would you like to have been a Forty-Niner? Why or why not?

   - Which group of people was treated most unfairly by the Americans in California? Explain.

   - Do you think the Gold Rush and other strikes were good for the country? Why or why not?

Assessment: Have students complete the Striking It Rich Quiz. Correct the quiz together.

Teacher Lesson Plans for Reading Comprehension *(cont.)*

Cowboy Life

Objective: Students will demonstrate fluency and comprehension in reading historically-based text.

Materials: copies of Cowboy Life (pages 28–30); copies of Cowboy Life Quiz (page 40); additional reading selections from books, encyclopedias, and Internet sources for enrichment

Procedure

1. Reproduce and distribute Cowboy Life. Review pre-reading skills by briefly reviewing the text and encouraging students to underline, make notes in the margins, write questions, and highlight unfamiliar words as they read.
2. Have students read the article independently, in small groups, or together as a class.
3. As a class, discuss the following questions or others of your choosing:
    *   Would you like to have been a cowboy or cowgirl? Give your reasons.
    *   What was the best thing about being a cowboy?
    *   What was the worst thing about being a cowboy?

Assessment: Have students complete the Cowboy Life Quiz. Correct the quiz together.

Native Americans

Objective: Students will demonstrate fluency and comprehension in reading historically-based text.

Materials: copies of Native Americans (pages 31–33); copies of Native Americans Quiz (page 41); additional reading selections from books, encyclopedias, and Internet sources for enrichment

Procedure

1. Reproduce and distribute Native Americans. Review pre-reading skills by briefly reviewing the text and encouraging students to underline, make notes in the margins, write questions, and highlight unfamiliar words as they read.
2. Have students read the article independently, in small groups, or together as a class.
3. As a class, discuss the following questions or others of your choosing:
    *   Who was treated worse in American history—Native Americans or African-Americans? Give your reasons.
    *   Which Native American tribe was most mistreated? Explain your answer.
    *   Which concept of land ownership do you believe in—the Native American viewpoint or the pioneers' beliefs?

Assessment: Have students complete the Native Americans Quiz. Correct the quiz together.

Reading Passages

The Westward Movement

A Series of Migrations

The Westward movement of the American people across the continent from the Atlantic colonies to the Pacific coast was one of the greatest migrations in human history. Millions of settlers, American-born and immigrants from other lands, moved from the original 13 states across the nation. They eventually reached the Pacific coastline, and some then backtracked to settle in the Great Plains in the center of the country.

Heading West

The first major movement away from the coastal colonies along the Atlantic Ocean began just as the nation was beginning to rebel against British rule. The Wilderness Road, blazed by Daniel Boone and his companions in 1775, provided a route for pioneers to get through the Appalachian Mountains. Migration into the Northwest Territory and the future midwestern states increased after the Revolutionary War and continued steadily into the 1840s. Settlers also moved southeast into what would become Alabama, Mississippi, and Florida when the Spanish gave up this land to the United States in 1819.

Manifest Destiny

Many Americans felt the nation had a Manifest Destiny, an obligation to expand and settle the continent from the Atlantic Ocean to the Pacific Ocean.

Expansion was seen as an irresistible historical tide. When Texas became an independent nation—separating from Mexico—settlers streamed into this new country and helped it become a state. The rush to Oregon and California began in the 1840s and continued for 20 years. Utah was settled in these years by Mormon emigrants. The last westward push was to the Great Plains, first thought of as useless desert and then drawing many farmers and settlers to its rich soil. By 1890 with the opening of Oklahoma to settlement, the American people had run out of frontiers.

Frontier Attitudes

The seemingly endless frontier of the nation's first hundred years shaped the ideas and attitudes of Americans in many important ways. People became movers. If things did not work out for a family in one territory, they simply gathered their belongings and moved on in search of richer soil, a nicer climate, or a better opportunity to succeed as farmers, craftsmen, or merchants. The idea of a chance to start over and create a new life was valued by most Americans.

 Reading Passages

The Westward Movement *(cont.)*

Do It Yourself

People on the frontier had no one to rely upon but themselves. They were separated from relatives and friends living in settled communities. These pioneers had to build their own homes and farms. They did the work themselves as a family unit and learned to be resourceful in meeting their needs. They built homes of logs, sod, or adobe depending on what was available. They treated themselves when sick because doctors were rarely available. Children learned to take responsibility early in life. They grew up quickly, married young, and raised large families.

Frontier Democracy

New frontiers were usually populated by poor people looking for a fresh start. The leaders they elected to run the government or local military forces were men of action who had not inherited land or wealth. Men like Andrew Jackson and Davy Crockett were elected to public office because they lived just as other pioneers did. Their followers admired the courage and success of men like these.

Leaders had to pay attention to the demands of their constituents if they wanted to be successful. This could be good because people felt an immediate connection with their government. It had negative results too. In many cases it led to legislation against Native Americans, minorities, and foreigners which restricted their lives and liberties.

The Role of Women

On the frontier, women worked beside their men. They endured the sufferings of the wagon train. They helped with farm work and ran the farm if the man of the family was injured or died. Wives helped build log cabins and sod houses. On occasion, women fought Indians and outlaws. They operated mills, stores, and inns. Although the father was considered the head of the family, the fact that they shared the work tended to give women influence in family decisions and a voice in community life. It is no accident that the first states where women achieved the right to vote were western states like Montana and Wyoming.

The Enduring Frontier

The frontier has lived on in American culture. In politics and government, leaders try to be inclusive of all segments of society as some frontier communities were. Americans admire individual strength and creative solutions to problems. Americans are still a mobile people, always looking for better opportunities to improve their lives.

 Reading Passages

Mountain Men

Fur Hat Fashions

A fashion fad in Europe and America in the early 1800s led to the origin of mountain men. Hats made from the thick fur of beavers became popular among wealthy men. Companies traded with Indians for furs in exchange for knives, rifles, blankets, and other goods. Some fur companies hired their own trappers, equipped them with supplies, and sent them to trap beavers in the streams of the far west.

Many Cultures

Mountain men came from the families of eastern farmers and merchants. They were the children of pioneers and the sons of immigrants. Many were French-Canadian fur trappers called *voyageurs*. Iroquois and Delaware Indians trapped in Oregon, and African-Americans roamed the Rockies. Even native Hawaiians were recruited as trappers by the trading companies. Some mountain men like Jedediah Smith were well read, and others like Kit Carson and Jim Bridger could not read a word. A few were very successful businessmen. Most of the mountain men lived from one trapping season to the next, dependent upon the price of beaver pelts.

Equipment

Mountain men were independent men who usually worked alone. They paid for their own supplies, which were quite expensive. A trapper needed a good rifle for protection as well as a large knife and a tomahawk. He carried a *possibles* bag made of buckskin, which held sewing gear, cooking tools, and other personal possessions. Mountain men used castor which was an oily, brown, liquid musk taken from the glands of dead beavers. They spread the castor like bait over their hidden traps to attract beavers.

Clothes

Mountain men usually dressed like their Native American neighbors in the wild country where they hunted and trapped. They wore rugged buckskin shirts, leggings, and moccasins. These clothes were warm and durable. Many mountain men also wore extremely distinctive and often colorful hats to demonstrate their individualism and be recognized by other mountain men.

Mountain Men *(cont.)*

Rendezvous

Fur companies organized places for trappers to meet and trade their beaver pelts for supplies, gold, and other things they needed. These yearly events were called *rendezvous* from a French word meaning "appointment or meeting." Mountain men lived and trapped by themselves for a year. They loved the rendezvous because they could talk to others, tell stories, gamble, and compete in wrestling contests, shooting events, and horse races.

Business

Trappers sold their pelts to the trading company for prices varying from $4 to $9 apiece. They often had several hundred pelts if they had been fortunate. The companies sold them supplies such as coffee, sugar, and tobacco at prices 10 and 20 times what the cost would be back east. Mountain men were able to make some profit, but they usually spent their extra money on betting, drink, and things they did not need.

End of an Era

The first rendezvous was held in the early 1820s and the last one in 1840. The fashion demands of the time changed, and beaver hats went out of style. Mountain men could no longer make a living trapping beaver, but they were resilient men. They had endured terrible winters and other harsh conditions in the wild as well as brutal battles with men and animals.

They had traveled and mapped large sections of the west in their minds if not always on paper. Mountain men sometimes lived with Indian tribes. Many died because of their dangerous occupation. Others became guides for government explorers or wagon trains. Some of the most famous mountain men are described on the following pages.

Joe Meek

Joe Meek went west at age 19 to become a trapper. He fought the Blackfoot and Bannock Indian tribes and married a Nez Perce girl. In his search for new beaver streams, he traveled the length of the Rocky Mountains from Canada to Mexico and as far west as California. He froze and starved, sometimes eating ants and grasshoppers and the soles of his moccasins. Eventually Joe Meek settled in Oregon with his wife and children.

Reading Passages

Mountain Men (cont.)

John Colter

John Colter was a member of the Lewis and Clark Expedition who was allowed to leave the expedition early so that he could join a group of beaver trappers. Colter wandered widely and explored the Yellowstone area although his fellow trappers thought he was lying when he told stories of water and steam bubbling out of the ground, smoking mud, and geysers. They called it "Colter's Hell."

Colter was captured by Blackfoot Indians who were very defensive about intruders in their land. They decided to have him run the gauntlet, racing between two rows of Indians armed with sticks and clubs who would beat him. If he escaped, they would chase him down and kill him. Colter surprised his captors with his speed and agility, dashing through the gauntlet and running away with the braves in hot pursuit. Colter managed to evade all but one brave. He fought him and then dove into the freezing Jefferson River and hid in a beaver lodge all day. At night Colter slipped out of the river and walked 300 miles in seven days to Fort Lisa, near present-day Omaha, Nebraska.

Jedediah Smith

Jedediah Smith was brought up in the eastern United States. As a young man he became a very skilled hunter and woodsman. When he read the journals of Lewis and Clark, he was anxious to see these lands and explore them himself. He was an unusual mountain man in that he was a quiet listener, carried a Bible with him, and read many books. In one of his earliest adventures as a fur trapper, he was attacked by a grizzly bear that mauled him and actually had his head in its jaws. Another trapper sewed Smith's ear back on and treated his wounds.

Smith explored more of the west than any other man of his time. He explored South Pass, the best route through the Rocky Mountains. Smith traveled through the Yellowstone area, across the Rockies, along the Platte, Snake, and Columbia Rivers, across the deserts of Nevada, and the length of California and Oregon among many other travels. He kept journals and maps but was killed before he could complete them.

Jim Beckwourth

Jim Beckwourth was a black mountain man who lived with the Crow Indians for many years and fought with them against their enemies, the Blackfoot and Cheyenne. He had several Indian wives and became an important chief and tribal advisor. He was a very successful fur trapper who tried to steer the energies of the Crow people into trapping and trading rather than constant warfare.

Reading Passages

Mountain Men *(cont.)*

Hugh Glass

Hugh Glass was possibly the toughest mountain man of all. He fought a grizzly bear with a Bowie knife and was torn to pieces and knocked unconscious. Two trappers who had agreed to stay with him until he died became frightened by the possibility of hostile Indians and took his belongings, leaving Hugh to die alone. Glass finally woke up and crawled to a river for water. Eating parts of a bison killed by wolves, other dead animals, and roots, he began a 200-mile journey walking and crawling across the plains to Fort Kiowa. Glass then hunted down the trappers who had abandoned him, although he did not kill them. Young Jim Bridger was one of those men who had left him.

Jim Bridger

Jim Bridger was a very young and inexperienced trapper when he left Hugh Glass to die. He went on to become the best known of the mountain men. He was respected by the many people he guided through the west, including army units and wagon trains. Bridger could not read his own name but he could draw a detailed map of every area he ever explored. He traveled widely through the Rocky Mountains and he was the first white trapper to discover the Great Salt Lake. He ran a trading company until the market for beaver pelts ended. Bridger built his own fort along the Oregon Trail. He mapped the best route for the Union Pacific Railroad through the Rocky Mountains.

Kit Carson

When he was 16, Kit Carson ran away from the saddle-making shop where he had been apprenticed. He worked on a traders' wagon train on the Santa Fe Trail until he made enough money to outfit himself and become a beaver trapper in the Rocky Mountains. He became a skilled trapper and explorer. Kit married an Arapaho girl and after her death was married to a Cheyenne woman. Both tribes respected his courage and honor. Carson was the chief guide for John C. Fremont's mapping expeditions in the 1840s. He was later an Indian agent and was trusted by the Native Americans he worked with.

Trails West

Reading Passages

Traveling West

There were several trails that pioneers could take on their journey west. Most were originally foot paths. These trails often followed rivers as much as possible to ensure there was water for people and animals. Most trails involved fording rivers, traveling through uninhabited or Indian territory, and crossing over rugged mountains. The journey was uncomfortable, physically demanding, and hazardous. It was definitely not a trip for the weak or faint-hearted.

The Gila Trail

The Gila Trail may be the oldest trail in the United States. Native American artifacts have been found on this trail that are 15,000 years old. The first explorer to follow this trail was Estevan the Black, a shipwrecked Spanish explorer who walked across much of the Southwest. Trappers and mountain men found beaver in the Gila River and used this trail.

Many Forty-Niners took this route to California although they were often attacked by Apache Indians. The trail begins in Santa Fe, New Mexico, and follows the Rio Grande and Gila Rivers. It crosses southwestern desert areas in Arizona and California and ends at San Diego, California.

The Wilderness Road

The Wilderness Road is the one of the oldest trails in the western United States. It was marked out in 1775 by Daniel Boone and a group of frontiersmen who wanted to find a route through the Cumberland Mountains. They began at the Holston River in Tennessee and followed the Cumberland Gap through the mountains into what is today central Kentucky. Boone and his fellow pioneers built a settlement called Boonesborough at the end of the trail near present-day Lexington, Kentucky. This rocky, rutted trail was for many years the only road through the Appalachian Mountains. By 1800 more than 200,000 frontier farmers had followed this road.

The National Road

The National Road was the first highway built with federal funds. Construction of the road began in Cumberland, Maryland, in 1811. By 1818 it had been completed to Wheeling, Virginia. Eventually it was pushed through Ohio to Vandalia, Indiana, not far from the Mississippi River. This was an essential route for settlement and commerce through the midsection of the new nation.

Reading
Passages

Trails West *(cont.)*

The Santa Fe Trail

The Santa Fe Trail was opened in 1821 by William Becknell. The trail began in Franklin, Missouri, which at that time was the town farthest west, and went to Cimarron, Kansas. Becknell did not think he could get over the mountains with his wagons so he took the Cimarron Cutoff, a route through the dry Cimarron Valley of Oklahoma. This short cut was dangerous because of the absence of water and the presence of hostile Comanche Indians.

Later, merchants often traveled in large caravans for safety. They started at Independence, Missouri, the new jumping off point for the Santa Fe Trail and the Oregon Trail. Merchants and settlers traveled across Kansas and followed the Arkansas River south. Here some travelers took the shorter Cimarron Cutoff. Others took the longer 900-mile mountain route to Bent's Fort, Colorado. There they turned south and crossed the Raton Pass and headed south. The two trails merged again, and all wagons traveled south through New Mexico into Santa Fe.

In the first 10 years, about 80 wagons and 150 people a year used the trail. These were mostly traders selling goods manufactured in the east such as cloth, pots, mirrors, and jewelry in exchange for furs, silver, horses, and gold. Travel increased in the late 1840s and 1850s. By 1860 some 3,000 wagons, 30,000 oxen and pack animals, and 9,000 people followed this trail each year.

The Old Spanish Trail

The Old Spanish Trail was an extension of the Santa Fe Trail from Santa Fe to Los Angeles, California. It was a regular route for trade between Mexico and California in the 1830s and 1840s. In 1841 John Rowland and William Workman led a group of emigrants from Santa Fe to Los Angeles along the trail.

There were two principal routes for this trail. One went northwest to Utah and then wound southwest to Los Angeles. Another route went through Durango, Colorado, across the Green River in Utah and the Colorado River and finally across the blistering hot Mojave Desert in Southern California.

The Oregon Trail

The Oregon Trail was opened in 1841 by a group of pioneers. There were 35 men, 5 women, and 10 children. They had no guide and no compass, but most of these travelers made it to either Oregon or California. The first major expeditions began in 1843 when more than 1,000 people, 120 wagons, and 3,500 cattle traveled west in wagon trains bound for Oregon or California. These numbers rose every year.

Reading Passages

Trails West *(cont.)*

The Oregon Trail *(cont.)*

Tens of thousands of people followed this route each year during the 1840s and 1850s. More than 300,000 emigrants used this 2,170-mile trail which stretched through Missouri, Kansas, Nebraska, Wyoming, Idaho, and Oregon. The Oregon Trail was also known as the Great Overland Trail, the Oregon Trace, and Emigrant Road.

The California Trail

Those going to California took the southern leg of the Oregon Trail, called the California Trail. The trail split about 40 miles past Fort Hall in eastern Idaho. Those who were California-bound traveled through what is now Utah past the Great Salt Lake, through deserts, and then along the Humboldt River. The exhausted travelers crossed 50 miles of waterless desert to the Truckee River. They then climbed up 70 miles passing through the Sierra Nevada Mountains and then down into the Sacramento Valley in California. There were several variants of this trail depending on when a wagon train split off from the Oregon Trail. Over 250,000 gold seekers and farmers followed the California Trail to California.

The Mormon Trail

The Mormons were a people with different religious beliefs who experienced persecution from the authorities and many of their neighbors in Missouri and Illinois. In 1844 their founding leader, Joseph Smith, was killed by a mob while he was in jail. The new leader, Brigham Young, decided to guide his followers west in search of a new home.

In 1846 Young led a group of 5,000 followers from a Mormon settlement in Nauvoo, Illinois, across what is now Iowa to Winter Quarters, a camp he established on the Missouri River in Nebraska. From there he led the first group of 143 men, 3 women, 2 children, and 72 wagons across Nebraska, Wyoming, and northern Utah to the Great Salt Lake Valley where he established a new settlement. Young organized permanent campsites along the route to help future emigrants.

Thousands of Mormons followed the trail from Nauvoo, Illinois, to the Great Salt Lake. Some farmers were wealthy enough to own wagons, oxen, and many possessions. Many less fortunate Mormons loaded all of their possessions into hand carts which they pulled and pushed for 1,200 miles across the plains, along and across the Platte River, and over the Rocky Mountains to the new settlement. Between 1846 and 1869, more than 70,000 people used the Mormon Trail.

 Reading Passages

On the Oregon Trail

Oregon Fever

Men who got the urge to travel into the unsettled regions of the far west were often said to have "Oregon fever." Many farmers and families were pulled toward the Oregon territory and other western lands by the descriptions they heard or read about from people who lived there or had seen the land. The attraction of practically free land rumored to be fertile and easy to farm lured many farmers, especially those with large families.

While most emigrants to the west recognized the dangers involved in the travel, the draw of land was incredibly strong. Some families had already moved across Ohio, Kentucky, Kansas, Missouri, and other states looking for better land. These pioneer farmers had been unsuccessful in farming where they had settled or were attracted to the lure of better land further west.

Economic Pressure

People traveled west for many reasons. Families often moved west because of economic circumstances. Squatters on land in some of the Midwestern territories had lost their land in legal disputes. Economic downturns, personal financial failures, debts owed to banks, rapidly rising land values (in states like Missouri), and the desire for a better life pushed families west. Some people just wanted to live in untamed lands away from laws and neighbors.

Reluctant Travelers

Men were the most eager to move west and brave the dangers on the trail. Wives and children were often much more reluctant to leave their family, friends, and communities. Women were more realistic about the dangers they and their families might encounter. They recognized that they would never see their aging parents or relatives again, and they worried about what would happen to their children if they and their spouse both died. Moving west was not a decision to be made in a hurry.

Pregnant Travelers

One out of every five women who traveled along the Oregon Trail was pregnant during some part of the journey. Giving birth along the route was more dangerous than at home. Most pregnant women worked every day on the trip right up to the time their babies were born. Sometimes the leaders would reluctantly stop for the day while a child was born. Sometimes the train went ahead, and the family had to catch up on their own. A pregnant woman got help from older women or other mothers during the delivery since there were no doctors.

 Reading Passages

On the Oregon Trail *(cont.)*

Accidents

Accidents were not uncommon on the long trip west. Some children fell or jumped off wagons, got caught under the wagon wheels, and were crushed to death before the oxen could stop. Wheels sometimes broke, and travelers were pinned under the wagons. Bison stampedes smashed wagons and hurt or killed pioneers. Riders were thrown when their horses were frightened or injured. Children and adults drowned in river crossings. Travelers were bitten by poisonous snakes on land and in water.

Wagons had to be unloaded and sometimes taken apart to climb mountain passes. Ropes were used to haul the wagons up the steep side of a mountain and then used to lower them down the other side. Ropes broke, and wagons crashed, injuring the men, women, and children who were pushing and pulling the wagons.

Disease

Disease and death were constant facts of life to everyone living in the 19th century, but life on the trail made the problems worse. Smallpox, cholera, and other contagious diseases killed travelers. Measles, scarlet fever, chicken pox, colds, and common childhood diseases were even more deadly on the trail because children and adults were already weakened by exhaustion, a poor diet, and close living conditions which spread the illnesses more quickly. Contaminated drinking water and poor hygiene also spread disease. All along the route, travelers saw the graves and the scattered bones of many men, women, and children who died on previous trips.

Native Americans

A few wagon trains were attacked by Native American tribes trying to keep the white settlers off their lands, but these conflicts were actually rare. More often Indians tried to threaten the travelers into leaving. A few natives stole horses or goods from the travelers. Only about four per cent of all trail deaths resulted from fighting with Indians. Accidents, disease, death in childbirth, and exhaustion caused many more deaths.

Rules of the Road

Most wagon trains elected a leader to settle disputes and make decisions for the good of the group. The leaders were chosen for their ability to make good decisions and get along with people, but often they had to make very tough choices. Families were told to unload some of their belongings so their wagon could keep up, and those who were holding up the wagon train by going too slowly were left behind. If a person had cholera or smallpox, their wagon was left behind in order to protect the rest of the group.

 Reading Passages

On the Oregon Trail (cont.)

The Route

On their journey west to Oregon, travelers "jumped off" from either Independence or St. Joseph, Missouri. From Independence they traveled the first 200 miles across the Great Plains to the Platte River, which they followed for the next 450 miles through what is now Nebraska and into Wyoming. Then they followed the Sweetwater River until it reached South Pass, the easiest route through the Rocky Mountains. West of the Rockies the trail followed a series of smaller rivers and streams until travelers reached the Snake River in Idaho.

Next the wagon trains climbed the rugged Blue Mountains on the eastern border of Oregon and followed the trail along the Columbia River for 200 miles until reaching The Dalles, where pioneers loaded their wagons onto rafts or Indian canoes.

Travelers then floated down the rapid and dangerous Columbia River, often losing all of their possessions at this final stage of the journey. After 1846 a wagon trail was used through the Cascade Mountains to the Willamette Valley. In both cases, however, the last leg of the journey was dangerous and often deadly.

Cut-offs and Frozen Passes

Some wagon trains hired guides who knew the route. Usually these were mountain men or adventurers who had traveled through the area before. Together the leaders and guides would choose the route to follow. Many wagon trains used guidebooks published by people who claimed to have traveled the routes, but these were frequently inaccurate.

Some wagon trains took cut-offs which were supposed to save days or weeks. Often these were much longer routes and cost travelers dearly in time and lives lost on waterless or dangerous trails.

The Donner Party

The Donner Party was one group of travelers that took a cut-off recommended in a guidebook. It got them to the Sierra Nevada Mountain passes so late that they were snowed in, and 34 members died from starvation after all of the animals and even leather harnesses and belts were eaten.

A few members resorted to cannibalism and ate members of the group who had died. The survivors crossed the mountains in deep snow, having lost everything they owned but their lives.

Reading Passages

On the Oregon Trail *(cont.)*

Early To Rise

On the journey to Oregon, sentries woke the camp with rifle fire at four o'clock. People crawled out of their wagons, tents, or blankets laid next to campfires. Families began their day loading the wagons, making breakfast, feeding the animals, milking cows, harnessing the oxen, and getting ready to move out by seven o'clock to beat some of the day's heat. The dust raised by the first wagons caused people in the rear of the train to be choked and blinded all day. Wagons usually took turns at the front so that everyone had some days with less dust.

Men drove the wagons, and some families rode the first part of the journey. As the animals tired, however, many men walked beside their animals or led them. Men also helped get the wagons across rivers, hunted for food, and did sentry duty to protect against attack by Indians. Mothers often walked, and children usually did. In fact, many children and adults walked the entire journey of over 2,000 miles.

Women cared for their children, mended clothing, cooked, and did laundry when they could. Children played with friends along the route, but they spent most of their time doing chores, caring for the animals, bringing water from rivers, and gathering dried bison manure, or droppings, to burn at the cook fires.

Celebrations

The weary travelers did have opportunities to celebrate. When they reached Independence Rock in Wyoming around July 4, they carved or painted their names on the rock, celebrated America's Independence Day, and rejoiced that they were almost half way through their journey. Weddings occurred on the journey as well because many teens found partners. Teenage girls often married as young as 15 years of age. These wedding parties involved feasting, dancing, and good-natured tricks played on the bride and groom.

Journey's End

Most of the travelers were extremely grateful for the journey to end. They were aware that they had achieved a great deal just by surviving the journey. These pioneers were exhausted but filled with hope. The new land seemed promising, and everyone looked forward to a fresh start in a new place.

 Reading Passages

Pioneer Life

Log Cabins

Pioneers who settled in wooded areas in the eastern United States or in the Oregon Territory usually built log cabins. This design was brought to America by some of the earliest Swedish settlers.

Frontiersmen spent weeks clearing an area for a cabin, cutting trees and removing stumps, brush, and rocks. Trees were cut to the proper length with an ax. Next, logs were smoothed and notched so that they would fit at the corners. Spaces between the logs were filled with clay or mud.

Some cabins had dirt floors, and others had log floors which were split and smoothed with an adz, an axlike tool. A fireplace was made with stones or sticks plastered with a thick coating of clay soil.

Glass was rare and expensive so many cabins had no windows. Others had windows which opened or closed like doors. The roof was the last part of the house to be built, and until it could be added, the cabin was covered with the tarpaulin from the wagon. A well was then dug near the cabin to provide water.

Sod Houses

There were no trees on the Great Plains so pioneers built their homes from chunks of sod, grass-covered earth, cut with a plow or an ax. Farmers stacked the sod to make the walls of the house. They used thin wooden sticks and brush as the frame for the roof. They plastered a layer of clay over the sticks and then covered the roof with sod, grass-side up. Many farmers dug their homes out of a hill or rise in the prairie. They left a thick layer of dirt and sod for the roof.

These sod houses were infested with mice and insects. The roofs usually leaked when it rained, and the floor became a muddy mess. During the dry season, dust was everywhere. The houses were dark, smelly, and uncomfortable.

One of the problems of pioneer life was the isolation. People usually lived a mile or more from their nearest neighbors. Some were even more remote.

The monotony of prairie life and the constant winds were especially hard on the women and children of the Great Plains who longed for companionship. As a result, some suffered mental breakdowns.

Pioneer Life *(cont.)*

Plowing the Land

To prepare the soil for planting, farmers used a plow. It was pulled by oxen or horses as the farmer walked along behind steering the plow. In the eastern United States, most farmers had cast iron plows which turned the soil easily. Poorer farmers had to make do with wooden plows.

On the western plains the sod was thick and hard to plow, but the invention of a better plow by John Deere made farming easier and more productive especially on the plains. The new plow cut through the sod easier, but it also left the soil loose to be blown away in dust storms.

Growing Crops

Farmers planted a variety of crops such as wheat, corn, potatoes, and garden vegetables. They raised cattle, sheep, horses, and chickens. Families tried to grow everything they would eat or wear. They also grew one cash crop they could sell for a profit, and they used the money from it to buy supplies and family necessities. Some years their wheat or corn crop would be successful, and prices would be high. In other years their crops were ruined by drought, fierce rains, hail storms, grasshoppers, prairie fire, or some other calamity. Sometimes farmers had a bumper crop, but prices were low because the supply was abundant so they made very little for all their hard work.

Farmers had little money and often bartered for the goods they needed by trading food or equipment. They had difficulty getting loans or credit because harvests were so uncertain. Farmers often lost their land to banks or the government if they could not pay back loans or pay the taxes due. Farming was a very tough, unpredictable business with many opportunities for failure.

Medical Care

Pioneers had little access to any medical care. Doctors were rare on the frontier, and medicine was not an advanced science. Mothers often gave birth to their children alone or with the help of a neighbor. Most pioneers had large families, often as large as 10 or 15 children, but many children died in childbirth or within the first year. Mothers were always at risk. Doctors often bled sick patients, a practice which only weakened the patient. Surgery was not advanced, and many serious wounds could not be treated. There were no medicines for the treatment of infection. A person either got better or died. Dentists were generally not available either, and teeth were usually pulled without painkillers.

Reading
Passages

Pioneer Life *(cont.)*

Disease

There were few effective treatments for the many illnesses that were common in the 1800s. Cholera was a deadly killer usually spread by drinking water or contact with a person who had it. Typhoid fever and typhus were common and often deadly. Smallpox killed or disfigured many. People got malaria (which they called "fever and ague") from mosquito bites, although they did not know the cause. Childhood diseases such as scarlet fever caused blindness, hearing loss, and sometimes death. Measles, whooping cough, and chicken pox could lead to long periods of illness and sometimes death.

Clothes

Clothes were a luxury on the frontier. No matter whether a family lived in the eastern woods, the western prairies, or the Oregon wilderness, they wore what they could get. From the wool of the sheep they raised, women made homespun clothes for the men and boys. This was a simple but durable cloth. A father and his sons might only have one extra change of clothing.

Most women and girls owned only two or three dresses at most and an undergarment called a petticoat. These were usually made by the mother from store-bought cloth. Children wore their clothing until it was nearly torn to shreds, and growing boys generally outgrew their clothes entirely before their mothers

could find the time to make a new shirt or trousers for them. Men wore hats and women wore sunbonnets to protect themselves from the scorching hot sun. Boys and girls went barefoot or wore moccasins. Women often went barefoot, too, saving their only pair of shoes to wear to church on Sunday. Men usually had boots or moccasins.

Household Chores

Pioneer families made soap out of ashes and animal fat. Roots, bark, and leaves were used to dye their clothes. Children living on the prairie gathered dried bison dung, old corn cobs, flower stalks, and dead grass to burn for the cook fire. Younger children fed the chickens, gathered eggs, and helped their mothers keep the houses clean.

By their early teens, children were plowing and cultivating the fields. They fed the animals, hauled water from the well or the creek, and harvested crops. During harvest time, the entire family worked from dawn to dusk gathering crops and storing them.

 Reading Passages

Pioneer Life *(cont.)*

Schooling

In pioneer times children went to school when they could. Settled communities quickly established a one-room schoolhouse. The school was just a log cabin with a dirt floor and a few supplies. Some schools, like those attended by Abraham Lincoln, were "blab schools" where everything was learned by memorizing what the teacher said or read.

Later students got a few books, but most used slates and chalk for writing. Paper and books were expensive. Children often shared readers and spellers. Students learning to read started with primers. Teachers focused on teaching the 3 R's—reading, writing, and arithmetic. Problems in arithmetic were based on the real-life needs of farmers and merchants.

Girls sat on one side of the schoolroom and boys on the other. Recesses were divided, too, with girls going out first and then the boys. A stove in the middle of the room provided heat against the bitter winters. Students of all ages and abilities were in the same room. The students' ages usually varied from 8 to 15. High school, or "the academy" as it was called, was often not available on the frontier.

Teachers were men when available, but the Gold Rush and "Western fever" lured men farther west. Many communities then hired young, unmarried girls to teach school. The girls had to quit when they married. Children attended school during the winter when they were not needed on the farm to do the planting and harvesting. Students often walked one to three miles to school.

Recreation

Recreation for the pioneers often centered on family and community events such as barn raisings, berry-picking outings, quilting bees, maple-syrup family gatherings, shooting contests, and corn-husking bees. Churches sponsored suppers and meetings. Weddings were a time for community celebration. Everyone enjoyed community dances where people of all ages danced. Pioneers celebrated holidays, especially Independence Day (July 4) with community picnics and speeches. In the wintertime, sleigh rides in the snow were popular and so were snowball fights.

24

 Reading Passages

Striking It Rich

Sutter's Mill

On the morning of January 24, 1848, James Marshall picked up a yellow rock near a sawmill he was building for John Sutter, a rancher who owned 50,000 acres of land in central California. Marshall and Sutter soon realized that they had found gold. At first the information was known only locally, but the news soon spread like wildfire throughout California, the country, and the world. By the summer of 1848, three out of every four men in San Francisco had left town to search for gold in the Sierra Nevada foothills. The miners quickly destroyed Sutter's land and the Native American villages in the area.

Forty-Niners

As the gold fever spread, men began to stream into California, which was pictured as a land where gold could literally be picked up off the ground. Two-thirds of the American men in Oregon went south to "strike it rich." News reports in September added to the excitement. President James Polk helped spread the news in his 1848 address to Congress.

In 1849 alone, almost 90,000 people—mostly men—set out for California. They came to be known as Forty-Niners. Tens of thousands journeyed for months on wagon trains across the country. Others traveled by ship. The sea voyage took three to six months whether they went around South America and sailed north or crossed the Panama jungle in Central America

and then sailed up the west coast to California. Either route involved seasickness, storms, poor food, illness, and for a few, death.

Within a decade almost 400,000 more people arrived from some 70 nations. Hawaiians, Chinese, Mexicans, Chileans, Europeans, and many others came to strike it rich. Freed American blacks and some Native Americans also prospected for gold. More than 1,000 black slaves were brought to California by their owners to help dig for gold.

Hunting for Gold

Forty-Niners soon found that the easy-to-find surface gold was gone. Miners used pans to separate gold from dirt and water. Those who could afford it operated a wooden rocker to separate the gold from worthless dirt and rock. Others set up sluices, or slides, across a bend in the river and washed dirt through them. Gold was so heavy it stayed on the bottom of the pan, rocker, or sluice when the water and dirt were washed away.

Sometimes miners found enough gold to keep them in supplies. More often, they found no gold at all. Thousands of Forty-Niners turned around and returned home with nothing but their lives to show for their efforts. Very few found enough gold to make them rich.

Reading Passages

Striking It Rich *(cont.)*

Merchants Strike It Rich

The most successful people never dug for gold. They took it from the miners. Merchants sold picks, shovels, mining pans, food, and other supplies to the miners at prices 10 to 20 times higher than normal.

A miner's wife named Luzena Wilson made a fortune feeding hungry miners at her inn. Saloon owners used gambling and drink to separate the miners from their gold dust.

Wah Lee, a Chinese man who opened a hand laundry, found his own gold mine washing shirts for the wealthy. Levi Strauss promoted a material he thought would be perfect for tents. It was not that great for tents, but the clothes he made from this denim material were very durable.

Strauss made his fortune selling pants, and today the pants he created are known as "Levis." Henry Wells and William Fargo set up a company that delivered mail and bought gold for cash. It became the most successful business in the West and today is the Wells Fargo Bank.

California's New Look

Before the Gold Rush, California had 14,000 non-native residents. Just three years later, it had 250,000 people—most of them men. The city of San Francisco grew from less than 1,000 to over 35,000 people. It had newspapers, hospitals, churches, and over 500 saloons. It also had 15 fire companies, which were desperately needed. The rapid growth led to crowded housing and frequent fires, many set by thugs. In 1850 California became the thirty-first U.S. state.

Trouble in Paradise

With the arrival of people from all over the world, many American miners began to try to push out the foreigners. The California state legislature even passed a tax of 20 dollars a month on all foreign miners. Many foreigners left because the tax was more than the gold they found.

There were 20,000 Chinese miners in California. For the most part, they paid the fee and stayed, but this led to violence against them. Their shacks and equipment were burned, and many Chinese were beaten or murdered.

Reading Passages

Striking It Rich *(cont.)*

Squeezed Out

Native Californios of Mexican ancestry often found their land grabbed by the newly arrived Americans. Although many Californios participated in the effort to achieve statehood, they often lost everything they owned. Native Americans were also pushed out of the mining fields. Their native hunting and fishing areas were destroyed, and thousands died from diseases brought by the whites. Native Americans of all ages were attacked, imprisoned, scalped, murdered, and driven from their lands. In 20 years' time, the Native American population in California dropped from 150,000 to 30,000.

The Comstock Lode

Gold was discovered elsewhere, too. In 1859 gold was found in Gold Hill, Colorado, near Denver. The rush there did not last long because the strike required deep mining. A wild rush called the Comstock Lode did occur in 1859 and 1860 in Virginia City, Nevada, when both gold and silver were found on the eastern slope of the Sierra Nevada mountain range. Miners rushed to Nevada from the camps in California where there was very little gold being found, but unfortunately the most successful mining here also involved digging deep into the mountains. Only a few men struck it really rich.

Other Strikes

A strike in Idaho from 1860 to 1862 was better for miners who washed gold out of streams. Gold was discovered in mountain valleys and gulches near Virginia City, Montana, in 1863. The Black Hills of South Dakota near Deadwood were the scene of a major gold rush in 1876. This rush caused major problems because the gold was found on land promised by a treaty to the Native Americans. Whites overran the area, and major conflicts broke out. The defeat of General George Custer and his troops at the Little Big Horn was a consequence of this gold strike.

The city of Tombstone, Arizona, had a silver strike in 1877 which lasted for several years, and rich ores were found near Cripple Creek, Colorado, in 1892. The last major gold rush occurred on the Klondike River in the Yukon Territory of Canada in 1897. More than 100,000 Americans set out in 1897 and 1898 for Dawson City in this desolate area. Gold discoveries were also made in nearby Alaska in 1899.

 Reading Passages

Cowboy Life

Wild Horses and Cattle

Cowboys got their jobs and their lifestyle because early Spanish explorers and settlers accidentally lost horses and cattle. These animals quickly adapted to life on the American plains.

The horses lived in bands of wild mustangs. Texas cowboys captured wild mustangs and rode them to herd and drive cattle.

The wild cattle were called longhorns, and they adapted to the Texas plains environment very successfully. The horns of a longhorn steer had a six-foot spread and were very sharp.

Longhorns fought off wolves, bears, and other natural enemies. They could live in very dry climates and endure freezing winter temperatures and brutal summer heat.

Birth of the Cattle Industry

Some Texans had started cattle ranching in the years before the Civil War, but it was not very profitable because there was not a big market for their beef. However, the end of the Civil War and the western expansion of the railroads led to the birth of a major cattle industry.

Ranchers hired cowboys to gather the cattle from the range in south Texas and drive them to cities in Kansas where the railroads had reached.

In 1867 an enterprising cattle dealer named Joseph McCoy bought land and set up a stockyard in Abilene, Kansas, near the railroad.

He then advertised in Texas newspapers to buy cattle. The response was quick. Herds totaling 35,000 cattle reached Abilene that year. By 1871 some 600,000 cattle were heading for the Kansas railroads.

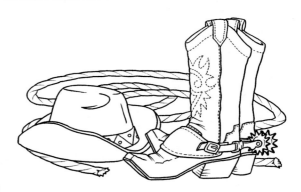

The Chisholm Trail

The first and most popular cattle trail was called the Chisholm Trail, a route used for years by an established trader named Jesse Chisholm. He helped survey several trails in Indian Territory.

Chisholm operated trading posts in Oklahoma and was respected and treated well by his Indian customers from many tribes. During the Civil War, he moved his family of 13 children—11 of them adopted—to Kansas.

The Chisholm Trail was 800 miles long. Cattle drivers followed this trail from Texas through Oklahoma into Kansas. The Goodnight-Loving Trail, which was used in later cattle drives, was over 1,000 miles long and went from central Texas through the New Mexico Territory and Colorado.

Reading Passages

Cowboy Life *(cont.)*

Cowboys

Cowboys were often boys, barely into their teens, who were hired by ranchers to round up wild cattle and drive them north. Even the promise of a market made the cattle business in south Texas an uncertain gamble, and the pay was poor. As many as one-third of the cowboys were Hispanic or African-Americans. These young boys, some teenagers, and a few older or experienced men gathered the cattle and drove them to Kansas.

Gathering Cattle

Cowboys worked from dawn to dusk. For weeks, cowboys gathered fiercely independent steers and ornery cows from the brush-filled ravines and open plains. They herded them on horseback or used a lariat to rope them. Cowboys were often pulled off their horses by the 1,000-pound steers that were as likely to attack a mounted rider as they were to run. Cowboys were gored by the angry cattle, thrown from their horses, dragged through thorny brush, and stomped by horses or cattle. They suffered broken bones and serious injuries and sometimes died as a result of accidents.

When the cattle were finally rounded up and kept in makeshift corrals, the men used a hot branding iron to burn the brand, or identifying mark, of their ranch into the hide of each animal. This proved the animal now belonged to that rancher.

Making the Drive

Some ranchers took all the cattle they could find on the drive. Most preferred to be selective and took four-year-old steers because these animals brought the highest prices. They also took cows and year-old calves which could be fattened or sold to northern ranchers. Newly born calves could not keep up and were killed if born on the trail.

When they were ready, the cowboys started herding the cattle north. This was difficult for the first two weeks because the cattle were anxious to return to the wild plains and often broke away from the herd. Then they had to be gathered back up. It took a few days before the cattle became accustomed to the drive. The lead steer was usually the toughest animal in the drive and the one that other cattle followed.

 Reading Passages

Cowboy Life *(cont.)*

Riding Trail

The trail boss, who was usually the most experienced cowboy, took the lead and scouted the trail ahead. The point rider rode in front and led the herd. Swing riders rode on the sides of the herd near the front and kept the cattle from going in the wrong direction. Flank riders rode behind along the sides of the herd. Drag riders were the least experienced and the most uncomfortable. They had to make the straggler cattle keep up, and they had to endure the dust from thousands of cattle.

Cookie was the man who drove the chuck wagon and cooked the meals. He was also the doctor when needed. Food might include beef but more often was beans, sourdough bread, and any kind of wild animal that might be killed along the way such as rattlesnakes, wild birds, or rabbits.

The horse wrangler and the horses used by the cowboys trailed the herd. The rancher usually provided the horses. Each of the 10 to 15 cowboys on a drive needed a string of about eight horses.

A herd traveled 10 to 12 miles a day on the drive. This gave them time to drink their fill of water, graze awhile so they would not lose weight on the trip, and then plod slowly along. A herd of 3,000 cattle might stretch more than a mile. The men stopped at noon to change horses and allow the cattle to drink. At night two cowboys rode herd around the cattle to keep them settled. They would often sing to quiet the cattle.

Stampedes and Troubles

Cattle were easily spooked and might stampede wildly in every direction. Lightning storms often resulted in stampedes. Bears, wolves, or unexpected dangers such as snakes or skunks could also set a herd off.

Gunfire and other loud noises could send cattle running over everything in their path. Cowboys often spent hours rounding up the cattle after a stampede.

Cowboys could be killed or injured during stampedes. River crossings were dangerous for men as well as beasts. Flash floods, poisonous cottonmouth snakes, and treacherous river bottoms all led to injuries and deaths.

The life of a cowboy was filled with danger, back-breaking labor, and adventure. The cowboys were grateful to complete their drives, which lasted three months or longer.

 Reading Passages

Native Americans

Struggle for a Continent

Native Americans were called "Indians" by the European settlers because the explorer Christopher Columbus thought he had reached the East Indies. The name stuck even after people realized that where Columbus had landed was an entirely new land. In fact, for centuries the Native Americans had lived in the area which is now the United States. They had adapted to the land and hunted, fished, and used only what they needed.

Tribes living in the Eastern woodlands with rich soil had raised corn, beans, squash, and other foods. Many tribes along the eastern coast of America had helped struggling colonists survive, but they soon learned that the white men intended to stay on their land and wanted more and more of it.

Land Ownership

White settlers from the eastern coast to the last frontiersmen of the Great Plains believed in land ownership by individuals. A person or family owned land, used it, and earned wealth from it. In contrast, Native Americans thought the earth, water, and sky were free to be used by all. Their tribe might claim a hunting area or tribal land, but it was for the use of the tribe and no one person or family owned it. To Native Americans, individual settlers took land, tore it up, ruined it for wild animals, and did not share with their neighbors—especially Native Americans.

A People Destroyed

Many Indians east of the Mississippi River were killed in conflicts or by disease. Entire tribal communities were wiped out. The U.S. government considered Indians a nuisance to be eliminated. The surviving Iroquois, one of the most powerful people in the New York area, had gone to Canada.

The few thousand remaining natives were forced to give up their lands and had to live on reservations in poverty. The remaining Algonquin people of the Midwest were forced onto reservations in Mississippi. At least 90,000 Native Americans were relocated.

The southern tribes were the most adaptable to white settlers' ways. The Cherokee were farmers. They had schools, mills, cattle, looms for making cloth, and a written language. Unfortunately, their acceptance of many "white" ways did not protect them or prepare them for what would happen.

Thousands of white settlers pushed onto their land in Georgia, and the state of Georgia simply said that the land no longer belonged to the Cherokee. The U.S. Supreme Court went along with this massive land grab.

Native Americans *(cont.)*

Trail of Tears

The federal government under President Andrew Jackson ordered the removal of the southern tribes to Indian Territory in what is now Oklahoma, more than a thousand miles west. This was a wilderness unsuited to farming, and the government did not think it would ever be wanted by white settlers. The Cherokee and neighboring tribes, including the Creek, the Choctaw, and the Chickasaw, gathered what they could carry and what wagons and animals they had and moved with the U.S. Army prodding them on.

The tribes endured dust storms in the summer and snow in the winter. They died from cholera, smallpox, and starvation on the way. At least 2,000 Native Americans, one-fourth of all the people on this forced march, died on what the Cherokee called the "Trail of Tears." Less than 60 years later, this new territory the Indians had been relocated to would also be opened to settlers, and most of the surviving Indians would be forced onto reservations on the worst remaining land.

The Great American Desert

At first white settlers just wanted to get through the Great Plains and get to Oregon and California. The Great Plains were referred to as the Great American Desert and was thought to be unsuitable for farming. However, after the settling of Oregon, pioneers began to eye the Great Plains. The Homestead Act of 1862 allowed men to settle up to 160 acres at little cost if they could live on the land and farm it for five years. Railroad developers received government land as part of their pay, and they sold this land to settlers.

The Great Plains Tribes

The Great Plains were home to village tribes such as the Mandan, Hidatsa, and Arikara. They often lived on bluffs or hills near rivers. The women planted squash, corn, pumpkins, sunflowers, and other vegetables.

The northern and western Great Plains were inhabited by nomadic tribes who were dependent upon the American bison (large, ox-like animals with a shaggy mane over the front part of their bodies, often incorrectly referred to as "buffalo") for food and their other needs. The Cheyenne, Arapaho, Blackfoot, Crow, and Sioux were some of the nomadic tribes. The Comanche and Kiowa were powerful nomadic tribes on the southern plains.

The lifestyle and power of the Plains Indians were greatly changed with the coming of the horse. Tribesmen learned to capture and ride these wild animals. Horses increased the Indians' ability to hunt bison and also made them much more effective warriors.

 Reading Passages

Native Americans *(cont.)*

The Last Bison

To the Plains tribes, the bison was everything. Bison provided food and skins for clothing and tipis. Their bones were used for tools and weapons. Every part of the animal was used in some way.

Before the coming of whites, these animals numbered 30 million or more. That soon changed. Hunters for the railroads killed the bison to feed the railroad workers. In addition, the demand for bison meat, bones, hides, and other products brought professional hunters to the West.

Thousands of American bison were killed each day, and the herds grew smaller. Many government officials, army leaders, and settlers saw the destruction of the bison as a way of destroying the Plains Indians and their way of life. They were right.

Indian Wars

The vast area of the Great Plains became the final battleground between white settlers and Native Americans. From the 1840s onward, Plains Indians fought a losing battle to keep the whites out. Settlers encroached on their land.

The United States government rarely honored the peace treaties it made. Tribes were constantly being forced to surrender more land.

The tribes sometimes had small victories like the Battle of Little Bighorn where General George Custer and 200 of his soldiers were killed, but the Plains Indians were outnumbered by the endless stream of settlers taking their land.

Settlers and some army units were involved in massacres of Native American tribes, sometimes killing Indian leaders like Black Kettle who were advocates of peace.

Tribes were beaten by an experienced, well-equipped army. The Nez Perce tribe, forced to fight to defend its remaining lands, was beaten. The Kiowa and the Comanche were ultimately forced onto reservations, and even the Apache accepted defeat. The Native Americans lost their land, their lives, and their cultures.

The Westward Movement Quiz

Directions: Read pages 8 and 9 about the Westward Movement. Answer each question below by circling the correct answer.

1. Through what mountains did the Wilderness Road provide a route?

   a. Appalachian

   b. Rockies

   c. Sierra Nevada

   d. Cascade

2. What term describes the idea that the United States would extend from the Atlantic to the Pacific Ocean?

   a. migration

   b. Manifest Destiny

   c. democracy

   d. immigration

3. Which man symbolizes a frontier leader?

   a. George Washington

   b. John Adams

   c. Davy Crockett

   d. Thomas Jefferson

4. Which of these materials was not used to build frontier homes?

   a. cement

   b. logs

   c. sod

   d. adobe

5. Which area was the last to be settled?

   a. Oregon

   b. California

   c. Ohio

   d. Oklahoma

6. Which of the following jobs did women do on the frontier?

   a. operated stores

   b. built cabins

   c. fought Indians

   d. all of the above

7. Which state was among the first to allow women to vote?

   a. New York

   b. Tennessee

   c. Montana

   d. California

8. Which of the following was generally true of young people on the frontier?

   a. They married young.

   b. They accepted responsibility.

   c. They played a lot.

   d. Both a and b

9. What does the word *constituents* mean?

   a. hunters

   b. voters

   c. miners

   d. politicians

10. When did the Spanish give Florida and parts of Alabama and Mississippi to the United States?

    a. 1819

    b. 1899

    c. 1776

    d. 1789

Mountain Men Quiz

Directions: Read pages 10–13 about the mountain men. Answer each question below by circling the correct answer.

1. What was the name given to French fur trappers?
   a. Iroquois
   b. possibles
   c. voyageurs
   d. rendezvous

2. Who explored more of the west than any other man of his time?
   a. Jim Beckwourth
   b. Jedediah Smith
   c. Andrew Jackson
   d. Hugh Glass

3. Which mountain man ran the gauntlet through the Blackfoot tribe and escaped from them?
   a. Hugh Glass
   b. Jedediah Smith
   c. John Colter
   d. Joe Meek

4. What is the name of an oily musk made from the glands of dead beavers?
   a. rendezvous
   b. castor
   c. trap
   d. buckskin

5. Which area did the mountain men call "Colter's Hell"?
   a. Nevada
   b. Rocky Mountains
   c. Mexico
   d. Yellowstone

6. What is the meaning of the word *rendezvous*?
   a. meeting
   b. war
   c. fur trapper
   d. trade

7. What animal did mountain men trap in the West?
   a. deer
   b. beavers
   c. mountain goats
   d. bears

8. What did mountain man usually wear?
   a. buckskin shirts
   b. moccasins
   c. distinctive hats
   d. all of the above

9. Which famous mountain man left Hugh Glass to die alone?
   a. Jim Bridger
   b. Thomas Jefferson
   c. Kit Carson
   d. Jedediah Smith

10. Who was the chief guide for John C. Fremont's mapping expeditions?
    a. Jedediah Smith
    b. Jim Beckwourth
    c. Kit Carson
    d. Jim Bridger

Trails West Quiz

Directions: Read pages 14–16 about the western trails. Answer each question below by circling the correct answer.

1. In what year was the Oregon Trail opened?

    a. 1865

    b. 1914

    c. 1841

    d. 1876

2. Which western trail was opened by William Becknell in 1821?

    a. Oregon Trail

    b. Gila Trail

    c. Old Spanish Trail

    d. Santa Fe Trail

3. Which trail guided more than 250,000 farmers and miners to California?

    a. Gila Trail

    b. Santa Fe Trail

    c. California Trail

    d. Mormon Trail

4. Which religious group led by Brigham Young moved west to escape persecution?

    a. Baptists

    b. Mormons

    c. Catholics

    d. Methodists

5. Which was the first highway built with federal funds?

    a. National Road

    b. Gila Trail

    c. Wilderness Road

    d. Old Spanish Trail

6. Which trail split off the Oregon Trail for those traveling to California?

    a. Santa Fe Trail

    b. Mormon Trail

    c. California Trail

    d. National Road

7. What does the word *merchant* mean?

    a. storekeeper

    b. explorer

    c. settler

    d. trail boss

8. Which trail was marked out by Daniel Boone?

    a. Oregon Trail

    b. Wilderness Road

    c. National Road

    d. Mormon Trail

9. What made travel westward dangerous?

    a. rugged mountains

    b. Indians

    c. poor hunting

    d. both a and b

10. Who led a wagon train along the Old Spanish Trail from Santa Fe to Los Angeles in 1841?

    a. Daniel Boone

    b. William Workman

    c. John Rowland

    d. both b and c

On the Oregon Trail Quiz

Directions: Read pages 17–20 about life on the Oregon Trail. Answer each question below by circling the correct answer.

1. What were people who traveled to the unsettled West said to have?

   a. cabin fever

   b. Oregon fever

   c. cannibalism

   d. contagion

2. Which of the following was least dangerous to travelers on the Oregon Trail?

   a. Indian tribes

   b. disease

   c. accidents

   d. exhaustion

3. Which word means a disease can be easily caught by other people?

   a. cannibalism

   b. exhaustion

   c. contagious

   d. fertile

4. Who were most eager to travel west?

   a. children

   b. women

   c. grandparents

   d. men

5. Why did families move to Oregon?

   a. financial failures

   b. debts owed to banks

   c. rising land values

   d. all of the above

6. Which is not a contagious disease?

   a. cholera

   b. scarlet fever

   c. snakebite

   d. smallpox

7. What happened to the Donner Party?

   a. They took a shortcut.

   b. They got snowed in.

   c. They resorted to cannibalism.

   d. all of the above

8. How long was the journey along the Oregon Trail?

   a. 200 miles

   b. 2,000 miles

   c. 20,000 miles

   d. 1,000 miles

9. What did the travelers burn in their cook fires?

   a. wood

   b. coal

   c. dried bison manure

   d. gas

10. At what time did wagon trains start off each morning?

    a. 9 o'clock

    b. 7 o'clock

    c. 6 o'clock

    d. 5 o'clock

Pioneer Life Quiz

Directions: Read pages 21–24 about pioneer life. Answer each question below by circling the correct answer.

1. What was a log cabin covered with before the roof was completed?
   a. sod
   b. dirt
   c. wagon tarpaulin
   d. plastic

2. What word means to trade for goods instead of using money?
   a. barter
   b. isolation
   c. drought
   d. monotony

3. What kinds of homes did farmers on the Great Plains build?
   a. log cabins
   b. brick homes
   c. tipis
   d. sod houses

4. What kind of events did pioneers have for recreation?
   a. quilting bees
   b. dances
   c. barn raisings
   d. all of the above

5. What kind of schools required memorizing and repeating what the teacher said or read?
   a. blab schools
   b. academies
   c. one-room schools
   d. girls' schools

6. Who invented a plow that cut through the tough prairie sod?
   a. prairie farmers
   b. Daniel Boone
   c. John Deere
   d. Native Americans

7. Which word indicates loneliness and not being around other people?
   a. companionship
   b. infection
   c. isolation
   d. infested

8. What did pioneer families make from ashes and animal fat?
   a. soap
   b. candles
   c. medicine
   d. dyes

9. Which of these was not a feature of pioneer schools?
   a. the 3 R's
   b. children used slates
   c. all students in one room
   d. summer school

10. Which was not a problem on the prairie?
    a. isolation
    b. bartering
    c. diseases
    d. medical care

Striking It Rich Quiz

Directions: Read pages 25–27 about the gold rushes during the Westward Movement. Answer each question below by circling the correct answer.

1. Who first discovered gold in California?

   a. James Polk

   b. James Marshall

   c. Levi Strauss

   d. Henry Wells

2. Who came to California to find gold?

   a. Americans

   b. Europeans

   c. Chinese

   d. all of the above

3. Who made the most money from the Gold Rush?

   a. miners

   b. merchants

   c. Californios

   d. cities

4. What happened to Native Americans in California?

   a. Their land was stolen.

   b. Their hunting grounds were destroyed.

   c. Many died of disease.

   d. all of the above

5. What was a result of the Gold Rush?

   a. Miners became rich.

   b. People came to the U.S. from around the world.

   c. War broke out.

   d. Californios got more land.

6. Where was the Comstock Lode?

   a. Canada

   b. Nevada

   c. Montana

   d. South Dakota

7. When did California become a state?

   a. 1849

   b. 1860

   c. 1850

   d. 1897

8. Which foreign miners paid to keep their claims in spite of violence against them?

   a. Chinese

   b. Native Americans

   c. Californios

   d. Europeans

9. What business did Levi Strauss start?

   a. cleaning shirts

   b. serving food

   c. making pants

   d. buying gold

10. Which of these tools was <u>not</u> used to separate gold from dirt, sand, and water?

    a. rockers

    b. metal pans

    c. sluices

    d. plows

Cowboy Life Quiz

Directions: Read pages 28–30 about the life of a cowboy. Answer each question below by circling the correct answer.

1. Where was the end of the trail for cattle drives from Texas?
   a. Tulsa, Oklahoma
   b. Abilene, Kansas
   c. San Diego, California
   d. St. Louis, Missouri

2. Which was the first and most popular cattle trail?
   a. Chisholm Trail
   b. Goodnight-Loving Trail
   c. Oregon Trail
   d. Santa Fe Trail

3. What are mustangs?
   a. cattle
   b. oxen
   c. cowboys
   d. horses

4. About how long did cattle drives last?
   a. 3 months
   b. 3 years
   c. 6 weeks
   d. 1 year

5. How many horses did each cowboy need?
   a. one
   b. two
   c. eight
   d. four

6. What food did cowboys generally not eat on the trail?
   a. beans
   b. sourdough bread
   c. wild animals
   d. beef

7. How many miles a day did a cattle herd travel?
   a. 10 to 12
   b. 18 to 20
   c. 2 to 3
   d. 50 to 100

8. Which of these was not a danger to cowboys on a cattle drive?
   a. poisonous snakes
   b. stampedes
   c. flash floods
   d. overeating

9. What are *longhorns*?
   a. cattle
   b. horses
   c. wild animals
   d. spears

10. Which of these was not a cause of cattle stampedes?
    a. lightning storms
    b. bears
    c. cowboys singing
    d. gunfire

Native Americans Quiz

Directions: Read pages 31–33 about Native Americans. Answer each question below by circling the correct answer.

1. Who believed that the earth and the sky were free to be used by all?

   a. Native Americans

   b. pioneers

   c. miners

   d. cowboys

2. What was the forced relocation of the Cherokee people called?

   a. Journey of Shame

   b. Little Big Horn

   c. Weeping Willow

   d. The Trail of Tears

3. What U.S. president ordered the relocation of the southern Indian tribes to Oklahoma?

   a. Abraham Lincoln

   b. George Washington

   c. Andrew Jackson

   d. Theodore Roosevelt

4. To Native Americans, what did white settlers do?

   a. took and tore up land

   b. killed off the bison

   c. did not share with neighbors

   d. all of the above

5. Which U.S. Army officer was killed along with 200 troops by the Plains Indians?

   a. George Custer

   b. Kit Carson

   c. William Sherman

   d. Ulysses Grant

6. What does *nomadic* mean?

   a. live in one place

   b. wandering

   c. violent

   d. live on farms

7. What was the most important animal to the Plains Indians?

   a. cow

   b. prairie dog

   c. bison

   d. deer

8. What animal increased the power of the Plains Indians?

   a. horses

   b. grizzly bears

   c. wolves

   d. longhorn cattle

9. Which Native American people had schools, farms, a written language, mills, and looms for making cloth?

   a. Blackfoot

   b. Crow

   c. Cherokee

   d. Iroquois

10. How many bison lived on the Great Plains before white men came?

    a. 200

    b. 30,000,000

    c. 9,000

    d. 3,000,000

Teacher Lesson Plans for Language Arts

Vocabulary

Objective: Students will learn to apply their language arts skills in vocabulary enrichment.

Materials: copies of Westward Ho! (page 45); copies of Gold Rush Word Search (page 46); copies of Cowboy Terms (page 47)

Procedure

1. Reproduce and distribute the activity pages on separate days: Westward Ho! (page 45), Gold Rush Word Search (page 46), and Cowboy Terms (page 47).

2. Review the terms, pronunciation, and directions with the class.

3. Have students complete the pages independently.

Assessment: Correct the vocabulary activity sheets together.

Literature

Objectives: Students will read and respond to a variety of historical fiction and biographical literature related to the Westward movement in the United States.

Materials: copies of Focus on Author Laura Ingalls Wilder (page 48); copies of The Laura Ingalls Wilder Saga (pages 49 and 50) and copies of the nine Little House books by Laura Ingalls Wilder listed on page 49; copies of The Rocky Ridge Series (page 51) and copies of the Rocky Ridge books by Roger Lea MacBride listed on page 51; copies of Tucket (page 52) and copies of the five Tucket books by Gary Paulsen listed on page 52; copies of Pioneer Diaries (pages 53 and 54) and copies of fictional pioneer diaries listed on page 53; copies of *Sarah, Plain and Tall* (page 55) and copies of the book *Sarah, Plain and Tall* and its sequels listed on page 55; copies of Pioneer Biographies (page 56) and copies of the biographies listed on page 56; copies of Scott O'Dell's Historical Novels (pages 57 and 58) and copies of O'Dell's novels about Indian heroines listed on page 57

NOTE: Most public and school libraries have copies of the books listed on the aforementioned pages.

Procedure

1. Reproduce and distribute Focus on Author Laura Ingalls Wilder (page 48). Read the text together, and discuss the author's life with the class. Students may be familiar with the television series "The Little House on the Prairie," which is an adaptation of Wilder's books.

2. Reproduce and distribute the Laura Ingalls Wilder Saga activity sheets (pages 49 and 50). Briefly review the nine books in the series, and allow students to select the one they wish to read. Since the books in this series get harder as Laura gets older, help students choose a book appropriate for their abilities. The books start off at an easy third-grade level with *Little House in the Big Woods*, and the last books in the series are at a high fifth-grade and early sixth-grade level. After reading one of the books, have students complete the book report form on page 50. As an extension, students can write an essay comparing and contrasting Laura's life to their own life.

Teacher Lesson Plans for Language Arts *(cont.)*

Literature *(cont.)*

Procedure *(cont.)*

3. Reproduce and distribute The Rocky Ridge Series (page 51). Have students select one of the books to read. When finished, have students give an oral book report to the class. As an alternative, students could make a brochure that includes a summary of the book, an illustration, and their recommendation.

4. Reproduce and distribute the Tucket activity sheet (page 52). Review what *conflict* and *resolution* are, giving examples so that students understand the concepts. (*Conflict* is "the problem which prompts the action in a story." The five main types of conflict are: man vs. himself, man vs. man, man vs. society, man vs. nature, and man vs. fate or God. *Resolution* is "how the conflict is solved.") Have students choose one of the books to read and then complete the assignment independently. Encourage students to share their responses with the class or small group.

5. Reproduce and distribute Pioneer Diaries (page 53) and the Pioneer Diary Evaluation activity sheet (page 54). Provide copies of the books listed on page 53 or other diaries about Westward expansion in the United States. Help students choose a book appropriate to their reading abilities and interests. As an extension, encourage students to start their own diary or journal.

6. Reproduce and distribute the *Sarah, Plain and Tall* activity sheet (page 55). Have students read the book *Sarah, Plain and Tall* and answer the Comprehension Questions on the page. As a class or in small groups, have students respond to the Discussion Questions.

7. Reproduce and distribute the Pioneer Biographies (page 56). Have students read one of the biographies listed on the page or other ones about American pioneers. Students should select books that match their abilities and interests. When finished, instruct students to complete the assignment and write a one-page essay about the person they read about.

8. Reproduce and distribute the Scott O'Dell's Historical Novels activity sheets (pages 57 and 58). Provide copies of O'Dell's novels (listed on page 57) for students to read. Help students choose books suitable for their abilities and interests. Have students complete the Story Outline on page 58 after reading the book they selected. Allow students to share their outlines with the class.

Assessment: Use student activity pages and class participation to assess student performance on the literature selections.

Teacher Lesson Plans for Language Arts *(cont.)*

Readers' Theater

Objective: Students will learn to use their voices effectively in dramatic reading.

Materials: copies of Readers' Theater Notes (page 59); copies of Readers' Theater: Hugh Glass Ain't Dead Yet (pages 60–62)

Procedure

1. Reproduce and distribute the Readers' Theater Notes. Review the basic concept of readers' theater with the class.

2. Reproduce and distribute Readers' Theater: Hugh Glass Ain't Dead Yet. (Remind students that some westerners used the slang word "ain't.")

3. Assign students to small groups, and allow time for them to practice reading the script together.

4. As an extension have students write their own Readers' Theater as suggested at the bottom of the Readers' Theater Notes (page 59). Assign a topic to each group, or let students choose their own. Allow time for them to create and practice their scripts.

5. Schedule class performances, perform the scripts for another class, or present the readers' theater for parents at a school open house or other special event.

Assessment: Base performance assessments on participants' pacing, volume, expression, and presentation. Student-created scripts should demonstrate general writing skills, dramatic tension, and a suitable plot.

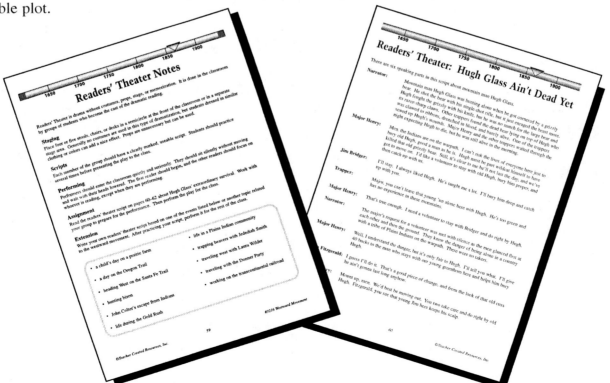

Westward Ho!

Directions: Match each term in the first column with its correct description in the second column. Use the glossary on page 93 or a dictionary to help you as needed.

Terms

_____ 1. cholera

_____ 2. Forty-Niners

_____ 3. gold fever

_____ 4. Great Plains

_____ 5. homestead

_____ 6. Manifest Destiny

_____ 7. massacre

_____ 8. moccasins

_____ 9. pelt

_____ 10. pioneer

_____ 11. reservation

_____ 12. sod house

_____ 13. tipi

_____ 14. transcontinental railroad

_____ 15. wagon train

Description

a. railroad connecting the U.S.

b. animal skin

c. the deliberate, merciless killing of many people

d. persons who went West looking for gold

e. a person who settles in a new area

f. tent home made of poles and animal hides

g. land set aside by the government for Native Americans

h. government land granted to families

i. desire to get rich

j. large land area in west central U.S.

k. the U.S.'s fate to settle the continent

l. group of covered wagons traveling together

m. disease gotten from drinking contaminated water

n. soft leather shoes

o. homes made from soil

Gold Rush Word Search

Directions: Find these words in the word search puzzle below.

Alaska	gold fever	merchants	shovels
Black Hills	immigrants	miners	silver
California	James Marshall	ore	stake a claim
Comstock Lode	James Polk	picks	strike it rich
Forty-Niners	John Sutter	San Francisco	Sutter's Mill

```
O M D E R A L A S K A K H S S
C S I M D B A L G P N C S L T
S I O N Y O E N I E I P T L A
I L W S E V L C Q R J O N I K
C V E R O R K K T X N I A H E
N E Y H F S S I C M I U H K A
A R S J A M E S P O L K C C C
R O J B V K I C C H T N R A L
F C A L I F O R N I A S E L A
N F O R T Y N I N E R S M B I
A B T R E T T U S N H O J O M
S S L L I M S R E T T U S O C
I M M I G R A N T S Y R R X N
R E V E F D L O G H U Y P R B
L L A H S R A M S E M A J W S
```

Cowboy Terms

Directions: Complete the crossword puzzle below using the terms listed below. Use the glossary on page 93 or a dictionary to help you if needed.

Word List

bandana	cattle rustler	lasso	spurs
beans	chaps	longhorns	stampede
branding iron	chuck wagon	mustangs	stirrup
bridle	corral	roundup	trail boss
bronco buster	horses	saddle	wrangler

Across
1. protective leggings
4. pointed wheels worn on boots
6. wild horses
8. burns an identifying mark on an animal's hide
9. type of cattle cowboys herded
10. fenced pen for cattle
11. head cowboy on a trail ride
13. horse trainer
15. place for cowboy's boot while on a horse
16. gathering cattle together
17. rope
18. padded leather seat put on a horse

Down
1. the food wagon
2. person who steals cows
3. large handkerchief
5. cowboy in charge of the horses
7. what cowboys ride
12. panicked animals running wild
13. harness for guiding a horse
14. food cowboys often ate

Focus on Author Laura Ingalls Wilder

Laura Ingalls Wilder was in her sixties when she decided to tell the story of her childhood. A true child of the frontier, she had traveled with her family across much of midwestern America looking for fertile land and a brighter future. A gifted writer with a clear, simple style, Laura's eight Little House books became immensely popular and have remained so for over 75 years.

Laura Elizabeth Ingalls was born to Charles and Caroline Ingalls on February 7, 1867, in a log cabin in the Wisconsin woods. She had an older sister named Mary. (Her younger sisters Carrie and Grace would be born later). A year after Laura's birth, the family moved to Missouri. However, they soon left for Kansas in hopes of filing a homestead on government land. Under the Homestead Act passed in 1862, a family that built a house and farmed 160 acres for five years would own the land. Unfortunately the land Pa (Laura's father) chose was on an Osage Indian Reservation, and the Ingalls family was forced to leave a year later.

The family returned to Wisconsin and then moved west to Walnut Grove, Minnesota, where they lived in a house dug out of dirt and sod while Laura's father built a wood-frame house and planted wheat. Grasshoppers destroyed the crops two years in a row. In school Laura met and clashed with a rival named Nellie Owens. The family moved again to an uncle's farm in eastern Minnesota where their newly born infant son died.

Laura's family moved on to Burr Oak, Iowa, and then moved back to Walnut Grove where they stayed a short time. In 1879 Laura's sister Mary suffered a stroke and became blind. Laura's aunt got Pa a job working on the railroad in the Dakota Territory where they moved and filed a homestead a few miles from De Smet, South Dakota. Here they suffered through the brutal winter of 1880–1881, which Laura describes in *The Long Winter*. A year later they were able to send Mary to a college for the blind.

Laura spent her teen years in De Smet where she attended school and clashed with a new teacher, Eliza Jane Wilder. Nonetheless, Laura became an excellent student and earned a teaching certificate when she was 15. She taught in small rural schools and later married Almanzo Wilder, the brother of her former teacher, in 1885.

Laura's early years of marriage are described in her book *The First Four Years*. The couple had a daughter named Rose and a son who died at birth. Laura and Almanzo faced many hardships. Almanzo was crippled by disease and exhaustion, their house burned down, and the crops failed. Eventually Laura and Almanzo moved to Missouri and settled on a farm in the Ozark Mountains where they lived for the rest of their lives. Laura died on February 10, 1957, at the age of 90.

The Laura Ingalls Wilder Saga

The Little House books written by Laura Ingalls Wilder are one of the most popular and famous series in children's literature. Laura was a frontier child who traveled by covered wagon with her pioneer family. This historical fiction series (described below in chronological order) is based on real events that actually happened to Laura and her family.

The Little House Books

Little House in the Big Woods. Harper, 1932. (Laura begins her story as a five-year-old living with her parents and older sister, Mary, in a log cabin in the Wisconsin woods.)

Farmer Boy. Harper, 1933. (This is a story of Almanzo Wilder's childhood living on a farm in northern New York State.)

Little House on the Prairie. Harper, 1935. (The Ingalls family builds a home and starts farming on the Kansas prairie until the government orders them off the land reserved for Osage Indians.)

On the Banks of Plum Creek. Harper, 1937. (The Ingalls move to Minnesota. Eight-year-old Laura goes to school, plays in the creek, and enjoys prairie life until a plague of grasshoppers changes the family's fortunes.)

By the Shores of Silver Lake. Harper, 1939. (Laura is 12, Mary has gone blind, and Pa works for the railroad while looking for a homestead in the Dakota Territory.)

The Long Winter. Harper, 1940. (Laura shows her endurance and strength as the family struggles to survive a seven-month winter of terrible blizzards and near starvation.)

Little Town on the Prairie. Harper, 1941. (Laura is 14 and working to help earn money to send Mary to a college for the blind. She makes new friends, competes with rival Nellie Oleson, and clashes with her new teacher Eliza Jane Wilder.)

These Happy Golden Years. Harper, 1943. (Laura is a 15-year-old teacher in a one-room schoolhouse with some problem children. Almanzo Wilder takes her back home every weekend.)

The First Four Years. Harper, 1971. (Published after her death, this is the story of Laura's first four years of marriage to Almanzo Wilder on their first homestead.)

The Laura Ingalls Wilder Saga *(cont.)*

Directions: Read one of the Little House books described on page 49. Then complete the form below and share your responses with the class or a small group.

Title of book: _____

Laura's age: _____

Setting (where Laura and her family live): _____

Laura's personality (Describe one event that shows what Laura is like.): _____

_____

_____

Important people in Laura's life: _____

_____

Pastimes (Describe two enjoyable activities that Laura does with her family or friends.):

1. _____

2. _____

Important events (Describe two important events that occurred in Laura's life.):

1. _____

2. _____

Problems (Describe two problems that Laura or her family faced.):

1. _____

2. _____

Extension

Write an essay comparing and contrasting Laura's pioneer lifestyle with your life in modern times. Include some of the following ideas in the essay.

- toys, games, and recreation
- farming methods and equipment
- school subjects and activities
- dangers, illnesses, and fears

- food and meal times
- means of travel
- children's chores and behavior
- clothing

The Rocky Ridge Series

Laura and Almanzo Wilder had one daughter, Rose, who became an author. Rose helped her mother organize some of the material for the Little House books and kept many papers and notes on her own childhood. She shared them and her memories with her adopted grandson, Roger Lea MacBride, who created a fictionalized account of Rose's childhood in a series of books written after her death. This Rocky Ridge series (listed below in chronological order) is a sequel to Laura's Little House books.

Little House on Rocky Ridge. HarperCollins, 1993. (In 1894 Laura, Almanzo, and seven-year-old Rose leave South Dakota and travel by covered wagon through Nebraska and Kansas to settle in a new, permanent home in Missouri which they call Rocky Ridge Farm.)

Little Farm in the Ozarks. HarperCollins, 1994. (Rose's family adopts two orphaned boys, and they try to make a living on the farm. Rose makes new friends, attends school, and manages to get into a little trouble.)

In the Land of the Big Red Apple. HarperCollins, 1995. (Rose's family gathers their first real harvest and celebrates a special Christmas. Abe falls in love, and Rose tells a terrible lie.)

On the Other Side of the Hill. HarperCollins, 1995. (A series of disasters makes life on the farm very difficult.)

Little Town in the Ozarks. HarperCollins, 1996. (Rose's family is forced to leave the farm, and Rose has trouble adjusting to life in town.)

New Dawn on Rocky Ridge. HarperCollins, 1997. (At the start of the 20th century, there is new hope for the success of the farm and 13-year-old Rose falls in love.)

On the Banks of the Bayou. HarperCollins, 1998. (Rose goes to live with her Aunt Eliza Jane in Louisiana while she attends school.)

Bachelor Girl. HarperCollins, 1999. (Rose leaves home to live and work in Kansas City and later in San Francisco.)

Assignment

Read one of the Rocky Ridge books listed above. Then give an oral report to the class. Include the following information:

- a brief summary of the story
- your favorite event in the book
- your opinion of Rose (Do you like her? Why or why not?)
- a description of one interesting character
- how this book differs from a Little House book
- your recommendation about the book

| 1650 | 1700 | 1750 | 1800 | 1850 | 1900 |

Tucket

Gary Paulsen is a popular author of children's books in the United States. Many of his books are based on his personal life. His experiences as a woodsman provide many of the details for his books *Hatchet*, *Brian's Return*, and *The River*. Each of the books in the Tucket series (described below in chronological order) is an exciting, fast-paced, fictional adventure with an accurate historical setting and details.

Mr. Tucket. Delacorte, 1994. (This book introduces Francis Tucket, a 14-year-old boy who is captured by Pawnee Indians and rescued by a one-armed mountain man named Jason Grimes.)

Call Me Francis Tucket. Delacorte, 1995. (Francis is on his own and still trying to find his parents and sister when he rescues Lottie and Billy, two orphaned children.)

Tucket's Ride. Delacorte, 1997. (Francis and the children get entangled in the Mexican War and captured by renegade Comancheros.)

Tucket's Gold. Delacorte, 1999. (Francis and the children are on the run from renegades when they find a treasure.)

Tucket's Home. Delacorte, 2000. (Francis, Lottie, and Billy encounter a British adventurer, murderous ex-soldiers, and Jason Grimes in their final adventure.)

Assignment

The Tucket books are filled with conflict—between Francis and Mr. Grimes, Indians, outlaws, nature, the orphans, and other people. In each book, Francis also faces conflict within himself as he makes uncomfortable decisions. Read one of the Tucket books listed above. Then describe three conflicts that occur in the book. Discuss your responses with the class or a small group.

Title of Book: _____

1. Conflict: _____

   Resolution: _____

2. Conflict: _____

   Resolution: _____

3. Conflict: _____

   Resolution: _____

Pioneer Diaries

The diaries listed below are fictional but are based on the lives of real people who traveled across the United States and started new lives in unsettled areas.

Assignment

Read one of the following diaries or another one that has a Western setting. Then complete the pioneer diary form on page 54 and share your responses with the class or a small group.

Fictional Diaries

Durbin, William. *The Journal of Sean Sullivan: A Transcontinental Railroad Worker.* Scholastic (My Name Is America), 1999. (This is the story of an Irish boy and his father helping to build the Union Pacific railroad.)

Gregory, Kristiana. *Across the Wide and Lonesome Prairie: The Oregon Trail Diary of Hattie Campbell.* Scholastic (Dear America), 1997. (A teenage girl tells of danger, death, fear, and hope on a wagon train bound for the Oregon Territory.)

Gregory, Kristiana. *Seeds of Hope: The Gold Rush Diary of Susanna Fairchild.* Scholastic (Dear America), 2001. (A 14-year-old girl writes about her family's journey to California in 1849 and their search for gold.)

Levine, Ellen. *The Journal of Jedediah Barstow: An Emigrant on the Oregon Trail.* Scholastic (My Name Is America), 2002. (An orphaned boy gains maturity and courage as he travels along the Oregon Trail.)

McDonald, Megan. *All the Stars in the Sky: The Santa Fe Trail Diary of Florrie Mack Ryder.* Scholastic (Dear America), 1997. (A girl traveling to a new home in Santa Fe makes friends with a Cheyenne girl, gets separated from her parents, and overcomes fear.)

Murphy, Jim. *My Face to the Wind: The Diary of Sarah Jane Price, a Prairie Teacher.* Scholastic (Dear America), 2001. (A young teacher records her experiences in the West in the 1880s.)

Murphy, Jim. *West to a Land of Plenty: The Diary of Teresa Angelino Viscardi.* Scholastic (Dear America), 1998. (This is a realistic, exciting account of two sisters and the many dangers they face traveling from New York to Idaho territory in 1883.)

Philbrick, Rodman. *The Journey of Douglas Allen Deeds: The Donner Party Expedition.* Scholastic (My Name Is America), 2001. (A 15-year-old orphan travels to California with the Donner Party, gets trapped in a snow-blocked mountain pass, and makes a desperate attempt to save himself and rescue the survivors.)

Rinaldi, Ann. *My Heart Is on the Ground: The Diary of Nannie Little Rose, a Sioux Girl.* Scholastic (Dear America), 1999. (A Native American girl tries to retain her tribal identity while learning how to survive in a white culture.)

Pioneer Diaries *(cont.)*

Directions: Use this form to tell about the diary you read.

Title of diary: _____

Person who wrote the diary

    Name, gender, and age: _____

    Character traits (courageous, fearful, daring, humble): _____

    _____

    Hopes and desires: _____

Setting (time and place): _____

Circumstances/situation (dangers/problems the diarist faced): _____

_____

Important characters in the diary (Give a brief description of each.)

    Family: _____

    Friends: _____

    Neighbors: _____

    Enemies: _____

Events

    Describe a happy or important event: _____

    _____

    Describe a sad event: _____

    _____

Impressions (Tell your impressions of the diary.): _____

_____

Extension

Start your own diary or journal. Try to record at least one entry each day. Use the following ideas to help you think of what to write.

- Tell about important people in your life.
- Describe important events that are happening in your life.
- Describe books you are reading which influence your thinking.
- Mention some of your hopes, dreams, and plans for the future.
- Tell about local, state, or world events that are affecting your life or that interest you.

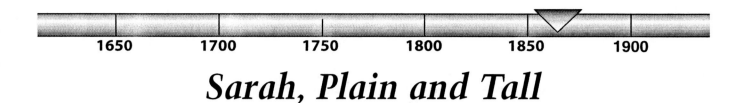

| 1650 | 1700 | 1750 | 1800 | 1850 | 1900 |

Sarah, Plain and Tall

Sarah, Plain and Tall is a Newbery Award-winning book by Patricia MacLachlan. It is the story of two motherless children living on the western prairie and the woman from Maine who answers their father's newspaper ad for a wife. The story is marked by gentle humor and genuine love.

Comprehension Questions

Read *Sarah, Plain and Tall*. On a separate sheet of paper, answer the following questions.

1. Who loved Sarah first?
2. How does Anna know that the chickens will not be eaten?
3. What does Sarah do with Caleb's cut hair?
4. What did Sarah bring from town?
5. What does "Ayuh" mean?
6. Why did Anna and Caleb want to know if Sarah sang?
7. What was the song about that Sarah taught the family?
8. Why did Sarah need colored pencils?
9. Why did Papa show Sarah the pile of hay?
10. Which neighbors came to visit?

Discussion Questions

Discuss the following questions with your class or small group.

1. Who most wanted Sarah to stay? Explain your answer.
2. What does Sarah imply when she describes herself as "plain and tall"?
3. What does Sarah miss the most about her former home?
4. How does Sarah demonstrate her independence as soon as she arrives?
5. What comments in the story tell the reader that the children miss their mother?
6. What are some of Sarah's actions that demonstrate her independent personality?
7. What are some of Sarah's actions that demonstrate her love of nature and of animals?
8. Do you think Sarah loves Caleb and Anna? (Give events from the story to support your opinion.)
9. Do you think Sarah was bothered by the storm? Why?
10. Would you place an ad in a newspaper for a wife or husband? Explain your reasons.

Extension

Read one of the sequels to *Sarah, Plain and Tall* listed below. Write a summary of the story.

MacLachlan, Patricia. *Caleb's Story*. HarperCollins, 2001.

MacLachlan, Patricia. *Skylark*. HarperCollins, 1994.

Pioneer Biographies

A *biography* is the written, life story of a person who actually lived. There are many biographies written about frontiersmen and women, cowboys, Native Americans, and other people of the American West.

Assignment

Read one of the biographies listed at the bottom of the page or another one approved by your teacher. Then write a one-page essay about the person you chose using the following questions as a guideline.

- What did this person accomplish in his or her life?
- What qualities (courage, loyalty, etc.) did this person demonstrate?
- What adventures did this person have?
- What dangers did this person face?
- What was the greatest challenge this person faced?
- Would you have liked to have known this person? Why or why not?)

Biographies of American Pioneers

Anderson, William. *Laura Ingalls Wilder: A Biography.* HarperCollins, 1992. (Good, basic account of the author's life)

Cox, Clinton. *The Forgotten Heroes: The Story of the Buffalo Soldiers.* Scholastic, 1993. (An account of the black Army soldiers who fought on the plains)

Eisenberg, Lisa. *The Story of Sitting Bull: Great Sioux Chief.* Dell, 1991. (Easy-to-read, detailed account of the great chief and his battles)

Faber, Harold. *John Charles Fremont: Pathfinder to the West.* Marshall Cavendish, 2003. (Excellent account of the life of the great explorer)

Fritz, Jean. *Bully for You, Teddy Roosevelt.* Putnam, 1991. (Amusing, easy-to-read biography of the "cowboy president")

Fritz, Jean. *Make Way for Sam Houston.* Putnam, 1986. (Well-written, humorous, easy-to-read account of the Texas leader)

Klausner, Janet. *Sequoyah's Gift: A Portrait of the Cherokee Leader.* HarperCollins, 1993. (Excellent account of the man who made a written alphabet for the Cherokee language)

Macy, Sue. *Bull's-Eye: A Photobiography of Annie Oakley.* National Geographic Society, 2001. (Great photographs and easy-to-read text)

Spies, Karen Bornemann. *Buffalo Bill Cody: Western Legend.* Enslow, 1998. (Easy-to-read account of the master showman)

1650   1700   1750   1800   1850   1900

Scott O'Dell's Historical Novels

Scott O'Dell wrote detailed, historically accurate novels for children that are based on real people and incidents which actually occurred. His books were carefully researched so that they reflect the lifestyle of the people he wrote about. Many of his books feature a Native American heroine.

Assignment

Read one of the Scott O'Dell books described below. Then complete the Story Outline on page 58.

Novels by Scott O'Dell

Island of the Blue Dolphins. Houghton, 1960. (A fascinating story of an Indian girl stranded alone on an island off of California for 18 years)

My Name is Not Angelica. Dell, 1989. (A slave girl in the Caribbean becomes involved in a revolt against slavery)

The Serpent Never Sleeps: A Novel of Jamestown and Pocahontas. Houghton, 1987. (The survival of Jamestown, the mistreatment of Native Americans, and the bittersweet love story of Pocahontas)

Sing Down the Moon. Houghton, 1970. (A Navajo girl's encounters with Spanish slavers and American soldiers who destroy her village and force her tribe onto a reservation)

Streams to the River, River to the Sea: A Novel of Sacagawea. Houghton, 1986. (An adventurous tale of Sacagawea's travels with the Lewis and Clark expedition)

Thunder Rolling in the Mountains. Houghton, 1992. (The story of the courageous Nez Perce efforts to escape from the U.S. army as told from the viewpoint of Chief Joseph's daughter)

Zia. Houghton, 1976. (Sequel to *Island of the Blue Dolphins*; Indians at the Santa Barbara mission revolt against the Spanish)

Scott O'Dell's Historical Novels *(cont.)*

Story Outline

Genre (historical fiction, fantasy): _____

Setting of the novel (where and when): _____

_____

Protagonist (name and two facts about the central character): _____

_____

_____

_____

Major characters (name and one descriptive fact about each): _____

_____

_____

Lesser characters (names and one descriptive fact about each): _____

_____

_____

Point of View (Is the novel told by first person or third person?): _____

Plot (the story in 4–6 sentences): _____

_____

_____

_____

_____

Problem/Conflict (the basic problem in one sentence): _____

_____

Resolution (how the novel ends): _____

_____

Feeling/Tone (book's general tone—uplifting, sad, funny, etc.): _____

_____

Theme (novel's main idea): _____

_____

Personal Evaluation (your response to the novel): _____

_____

Readers' Theater Notes

Readers' Theater is drama without costumes, props, stage, or memorization. It is done in the classroom by groups of students who become the cast of the dramatic reading.

Staging

Place four or five stools, chairs, or desks in a semicircle at the front of the classroom or in a separate stage area. Generally no costumes are used in this type of dramatization, but students dressed in similar clothing or colors can add a nice effect. Props are unnecessary but can be used.

Scripts

Each member of the group should have a clearly marked, useable script. Students should practice several times before presenting the play to the class.

Performing

Performers should enter the classroom quietly and seriously. They should sit silently without moving and wait with their heads lowered. The first reader should begin, and the other readers should focus on whoever is reading, except when they are performing.

Assignment

Read the readers' theater script on pages 60–62 about Hugh Glass' extraordinary survival. Work with your group to prepare for the performance. Then perform the play for the class.

Extension

Write your own readers' theater script based on one of the events listed below or another topic related to the westward movement. After practicing your script, perform it for the rest of the class.

- a child's day on a prairie farm
- a day on the Oregon Trail
- heading West on the Santa Fe Trail
- hunting bison
- John Colter's escape from Indians
- life during the Gold Rush

- life in a Plains Indian community
- trapping beavers with Jedediah Smith
- traveling west with Laura Wilder
- traveling with the Donner Party
- working on the transcontinental railroad

Readers' Theater: Hugh Glass Ain't Dead Yet

There are six speaking parts in this script about mountain man Hugh Glass.

Narrator: Mountain man Hugh Glass was hunting alone when he got cornered by a grizzly bear. He shot the bear with his single-shot rifle, but it just enraged the beast more. Hugh fought the grizzly with his knife, but he was no match for the large bear and its razor-sharp claws. Other trappers found the dead bear lying on top of Hugh who was clawed to ribbons, drenched in blood, and barely alive. One of the trappers sewed up Hugh's wounds. Major Henry and the other trappers waited through the night expecting Hugh to die, but he was still alive in the morning.

Major Henry: Men, the Indians are on the warpath. I can't risk the lives of everyone here just to bury old Hugh, good a man as he is. Hugh must be part wildcat himself to have killed that old grizzly bear. Still, it's clear to me he'll not last the day, and we've got to move on. I'd like a volunteer to stay with old Hugh, bury him proper, and then catch up with us.

Jim Bridger: I'll stay. I always liked Hugh. He's taught me a lot. I'll bury him deep and catch up with you.

Trapper: Major, you can't leave that young 'un alone here with Hugh. He's too green and has no experience in these mountains.

Major Henry: That's true enough. I need a volunteer to stay with Bridger and do right by Hugh.

Narrator: The major's request for a volunteer was met with silence as the men glanced first at each other and then the ground. They knew the danger of being alone in a country with a tribe of Plains Indians on the warpath. There were no takers.

Major Henry: Well, I understand the danger, but it's only fair to Hugh. I'll tell you what. I'll give 40 bucks to the man who stays with our young greenhorn here and helps him bury Hugh.

John Fitzgerald: I guess I'll do it. That's a good piece of change, and from the look of that old cuss he ain't gonna last long anyhow.

Major Henry: Mount up, men. We'd best be moving out. You two take care and do right by old Hugh.

Readers' Theater: Hugh Glass Ain't Dead Yet *(cont.)*

Narrator: Major Henry and the rest of the trappers left. Jim Bridger busied himself trying to make Hugh comfortable. Fitzgerald started pacing about the camp and checking the area for signs of Indians. The two were still there at nightfall. Hugh Glass was still alive, but each raspy breath he took seemed like it was the last one he would ever draw.

John Fitzgerald: What's that matter with that old man? He ought to be dead by now. It's nigh onto dark, and I can feel trouble. We should've been done gone by now.

Jim Bridger: Hugh's still breathing. We said we'd stay till he passed on.

John Fitzgerald: He's the same as dead. That old man's never gonna move from where he's lying. I tell you, we need to leave whilst we can.

Jim Bridger: He'll be dead by morning. We can do our duty by him and then move on.

Narrator: But Hugh was not dead by morning. He was still barely breathing, but Fitzgerald could not stand it anymore.

John Fitzgerald: We need to go. We're fools to stay here. The man's dead as a corpse. He just doesn't know it yet.

Jim Bridger: I reckon you're right, but what will we do with old Hugh?

John Fitzgerald: You take his rifle and skinning knife. I'll take his possibles bag. He's got some good traps and stuff. Make him comfortable, and let's go. Time's a 'wasting. We'll tell the others Hugh died and we buried him. Nobody'll be the wiser.

Narrator: They caught up with the others in a few days and reported Hugh's death, but Hugh Glass didn't die. He lay a few days in his half-conscious state and then woke up one evening to find himself alone, coated in blood, starving, and parched with thirst.

Hugh Glass: The Major left young Bridger and Fitzgerald to bury me. I heard him. Where did those two rascals go? Where's my rifle? My knife's missing, too, and my possibles bag is gone. They done took everything and skedaddled. Figured I was dead, they did. Well, I'll show them. Old Hugh ain't dead!

Readers' Theater: Hugh Glass Ain't Dead Yet *(cont.)*

Narrator: Unable to walk or even stand up, Hugh crawled down to a stream, drank all he could, and started crawling southeast in the direction of Fort Lisa. He found a dead bison which had been mostly eaten by wolves. He ate some of the rotten carcass, took some of the bones to gnaw out the marrow, and crawled on.

Hugh Glass: Be lucky to make a mile tonight. I'll chew out the bone tomorrow. I'll sleep during the day. It ain't but a hundred miles to Fort Lisa. I'll make it if'n the wolves or buzzards don't get me. And those two buzzards that left me to die, you just wait 'till I catch your hides.

Narrator: Hugh Glass slept during the day and crawled at night. He ate anything dead he could find and licked water from the underside of leaves and small pools of water that he found along the way. Weeks later he crawled into Fort Lisa. Hugh spent months there recovering his strength and remembering his promise to himself about the men who left him. Hugh left Fort Lisa with a borrowed rifle and supplies, following a rumor that Jim Bridger was trapping on his own on the Northern Plains. He sneaked up on Bridger's camp months later while Jim was cooking dinner.

Hugh Glass: Freeze, you yellow-bellied coward! I got you now!

Jim Bridger: Who? What do you want? Who are you?

Hugh Glass: Scared you, didn't I? Don't you recognize Old Hugh?

Jim Bridger: You can't be! Hugh Glass is dead! You must be a spirit!

Hugh Glass: I ain't dead yet. No thanks to you! Left me to die, you did. Yellow-dog coward!

Jim Bridger: But you were near dead. That old grizzly bear had clawed you up something fierce! You was bleeding from a dozen cuts, but you just kept breathing. I'm sorry, Hugh. I deserve to die, I guess. Go ahead and get it done.

Hugh Glass: I ain't gonna kill you—much as you deserve it. I'm taking your age into account. Young folks tend to do stupid things right often. You'll learn if you get any older.

Narrator: Hugh Glass never caught up to John Fitzgerald. He just disappeared and was never seen again. Jim Bridger, however, went on to become one of the most famous mountain men—a man who was highly respected for his courage and for keeping his word.

| 1650 | 1700 | 1750 | 1800 | 1850 | 1900 |

Teacher Lesson Plans for Social Studies

Using Time Lines

Objectives: Students will learn to derive and use information on a time line and add relevant information to a time line.

Materials: copies of Westward Expansion Time Line (pages 65 and 66); reference materials including books, encyclopedias, almanacs, and Internet sites

Procedure

1. Collect reference materials so that students can use them to find information.
2. Review the concept of a time line. Draw a time line on the board using events from the current school year as examples.
3. Reproduce and distribute the Westward Expansion Time Line. Review the events listed on the time line.
4. Instruct students to complete the assignment on page 66, adding dates to the time line and illustrating one of those events. Display these illustrations in chronological order on a classroom wall or bulletin board.

Assessment: Assess students' ability to research information. Verify the accuracy of the events and dates that students added to the time line.

Using Maps

Objective: Students will derive and learn to use information from maps.

Materials: copies of The Travels of Jedediah Smith (page 67); copies of Western Trails Map (pages 68 and 69); copies of Map of Native American Tribes (page 70); copies of U.S. Expansion Map (page 71); copies of Frontier Railroads Map (page 72); atlases, almanacs, and other maps for reference and comparison

Procedure

1. Reproduce and distribute The Travels of Jedediah Smith (page 67). Discuss the map with students, and then assign the activity on the page.
2. Reproduce and distribute the Western Trails Map (pages 68 and 69). Review the map, and instruct students to use the map to answer the questions on page 69.
3. Reproduce and distribute the Map of Native American Tribes (page 70). Assign the activity on the page.
4. Reproduce and distribute the U.S. Expansion Map (page 71). Tell students to use the map to answer the questions on the page.
5. Reproduce and distribute the Frontier Railroads Map (page 72). Instruct students to complete the map activity on the page.

Assessment: Correct the map activity pages together. Check for understanding and review basic concepts as needed.

Teacher Lesson Plans for Social Studies *(cont.)*

Researching the Westward Movement

Objectives: Students will develop skills in finding, organizing, and presenting research information.

Materials: copies of Who Am I? (page 73); copies of Researching Frontier States (page 74); copies of Researching Native American Tribes (page 75); copies of Become a Famous Westerner (pages 76 and 77); copies of Famous Westerners (page 78); books, encyclopedias, and Internet sources

Procedure

1. Reproduce and distribute Who Am I? (page 73) and Famous Westerners (page 78). Instruct students to use the Famous Westerners page to help them find answers to the Who Am I? activity sheet.

2. Reproduce and distribute Researching Frontier States (page 74). Discuss the assignment, and review with students the Writing a Report information at the bottom of the page. Stress how to find appropriate reference material, the need to take notes in an organized manner, and the information that students should find out about the state they choose. Assign a state to each student, or allow them to work with a partner. As an alternative, students could prepare a PowerPoint presentation on the state instead of writing a report.

3. Reproduce and distribute Researching Native American Tribes (page 75). Review the assignment and type of information they should find. Allow students to choose a tribe to research. If desired, students could work in groups with each student having to research a different aspect—lifestyle, clothing, homes, or food—about the tribe.

4. Reproduce and distribute Become a Famous Westerner (pages 76 and 77) and Famous Westerners (page 78). Review with students the assignment, helpful hints, and biographical outline. Let each student select a person from the list on page 78 (or choose another Westerner with teacher approval).

NOTE: Allow time for students to prepare their written and oral reports (described in steps 2–4 above). Arrange a class schedule so students can share their reports and presentations with the class.

Assessment: Correct the Who Am I? activity sheet together. To correct and assess students' written reports on frontier states and Native American tribes, use standard language arts guidelines. For students' oral presentations as famous Westerners, use the following rubric.

- General Knowledge (50%)
- Voice (Loud/Clear) 20%
- Dramatic Skill (10%)
- Costume (10%)
- Notes (10%)

Westward Expansion Time Line

1775 – Daniel Boone opens the Wilderness Road to Kentucky.

1776 – The Declaration of Independence is signed.

1803 – President Thomas Jefferson arranges the Louisiana Purchase, doubling the size of the U.S.

1804 – Meriwether Lewis and William Clark begin a two-year expedition to explore the Louisiana Purchase.

1806 – Zebulon Pike explores Colorado.

1807 – John Colter explores the Rockies and Yellowstone area.

1811 – Construction of the National Road begins.

1821 – William Becknell opens the Santa Fe Trail.

1825 – Jim Bridger explores the area of Great Salt Lake.

1827 – Jedediah Smith explores a southern route to California.

1836 – Texas wins its independence after the defeat at the Alamo and victory at the Battle of San Jacinto.

1838 – The Cherokee are forcibly removed from their lands and begin their Trail of Tears to the Oklahoma Indian Territory.

1841 – The first wagon train follows the Oregon Trail to Oregon and California.

1842 – John C. Fremont begins his first of three expeditions to explore and map the West.

1843 – The first major wagon train on the Oregon Trail carries settlers to Oregon and California.

1844 – Joseph Smith, the founder of Mormonism, is killed.

1845 – Texas becomes the 28th state.

1846 – The U.S. and Mexico go to war.
  – Britain gives the U.S. the southern part of the Oregon territory.
  – The Donner Party is trapped by snow in the Sierra Nevada mountain range.
  – Mormons move along the Mormon Trail to a new settlement near the Great Salt Lake.

1848 – The United States acquires California and the Southwest from Mexico.
  – Gold is discovered at Sutter's Mill in California, setting off a major gold rush.
  – The first stagecoach line to the west coast begins.

1850 – California becomes the 31st state.

1851 – Native American tribes agree to the Fort Laramie Treaty, which gives them the Great Plains.

1853 – The Gadsden Purchase establishes the final boundaries of the continental United States.

1858 – The first overland mail service begins from the west coast to St. Louis and the East.

1859 – Oregon becomes a state.
  – Silver is discovered in the Comstock Lode in Nevada.

1860 – The Pony Express begins mail operations in the West.

Westward Expansion Time Line *(cont.)*

1861 — The U.S. Civil War starts with firing on Fort Sumter.

     — The telegraph connects the east coast of the United States with the West.

1862 — The Homestead Act opens the Great Plains to settlement.

1864 — John Chivington leads 700 volunteers in a massacre of Cheyenne and Arapaho Indians at Sand Creek, Colorado.

1865 — The first railroad train robbery occurs in Ohio.

1866 — Jesse James leads the first bank robbery in the U.S.

1867 — The first cattle herds reach Abilene, Kansas.

     — The United States buys Alaska from Russia for $7.2 million (about 2 cents an acre).

1869 — First women's suffrage rights are granted to residents in Wyoming Territory.

     — The transcontinental railroad connecting California to the eastern United States is completed.

1876 — A major gold rush happens in the Black Hills of South Dakota.

     — General George Custer and his entire troops are killed at the Battle of the Little Bighorn in southeast Montana.

1881 — The infamous gunfight at the O.K. Corral is fought between the Earps and the Clantons.

     — Helen Hunt Jackson's book *A Century of Dishonor* details the mistreatment of Native Americans.

1883 — Buffalo Bill Cody starts his Wild West Show.

     — Sarah Winnemucca publishes the first book by a Native American woman.

1886 — Geronimo and his Apache warriors surrender to the U.S. Army.

1887 — Chief Joseph of the Nez Perce surrenders to the U.S. Army after a heroic effort to escape the reservation.

1889 — An Oklahoma land rush leads to the settling of the last frontier in the U.S.

1890 — Sioux Chief Sitting Bull is killed in a skirmish with soldiers.

     — The massacre of Native Americans by U.S. Army occurs at Wounded Knee Creek, South Dakota.

1892 — A Crow Indian reservation of almost two million acres is opened to white settlers by presidential order.

1897 — Gold is discovered in the Yukon in Alaska.

1898 — The United States annexes Hawaii.

Assignment

Find at least 10 dates in American history to add to the above time line. These dates could include the birth of famous pioneers, when states were admitted to the Union, Indian battles, inventions, presidential elections, natural disasters, or other events. Then choose one of these events to illustrate, color, and label on a separate sheet of paper. Be sure to include the date.

The Travels of Jedediah Smith

Directions: Jedediah Smith was the most traveled of the mountain men. The map below shows his wanderings and explorations between 1823 and 1830. Use the map to answer the questions at the bottom of the page.

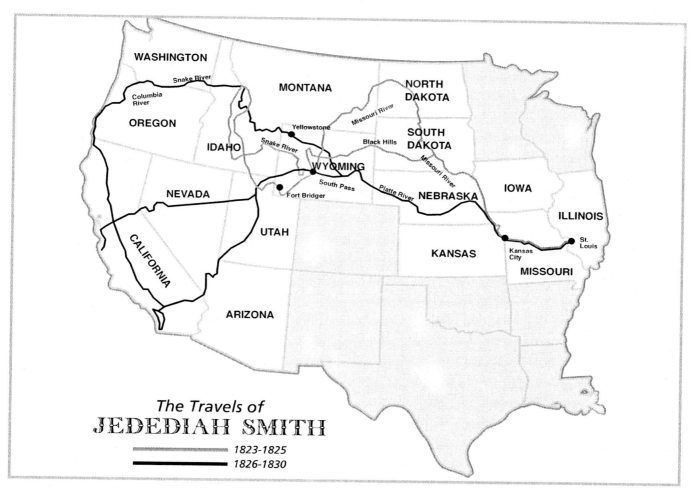

The Travels of
JEDEDIAH SMITH
1823-1825
1826-1830

Jedediah Smith viewed the following natural features on his journeys. In what state is each of these located?

1. Black Hills _____

2. Columbia River _____

3. Missouri River _____

4. Platte River _____

5. Snake River _____

6. South Pass _____

7. Through which of the labeled states did Jedediah Smith travel?

_____

Western Trails Map

The map below shows the trails that were used to travel west across the United States. Use this map to answer the questions on the next page.

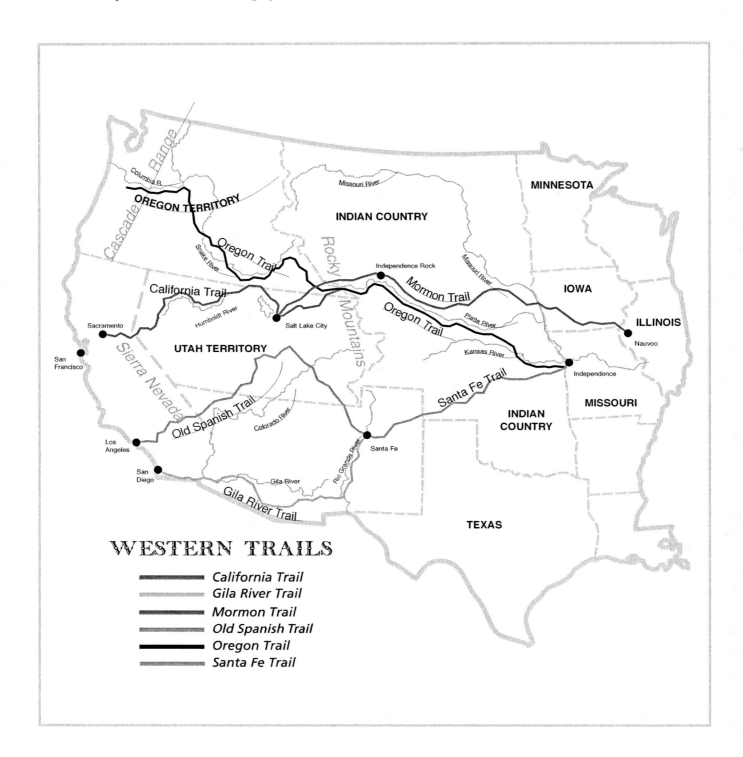

Western Trails Map *(cont.)*

Directions: Use the map on the previous page to answer the questions below.

1. What are the six major trails used for the westward migration of the American people?

   _____

2. Which city was the starting point for most of the trails? _____

3. In which two states did most of the trails end? _____

4. Where did the Mormon Trail begin? _____

5. Where did the Mormon Trail end? _____

6. Which trail went from Santa Fe to Los Angeles? _____

7. Which trail went from Santa Fe to San Diego? _____

8. Which trail was the longest? _____

9. Which western mountain range did the California Trail cross? _____

10. Which two trails crossed the Rio Grande River? _____

11. Which trail followed the Humboldt River part of the way? _____

12. Which trail went over the Cascade mountain range? _____

13. Which trail went over the Sierra Nevada mountain range? _____

14. Which two trails followed the Platte River for a long distance? _____

   _____

Map of Native American Tribes

The map below shows the location of Native American tribes in terms of present-day state boundaries. Where tribes lived changed, depending upon circumstances such as hunting and war.

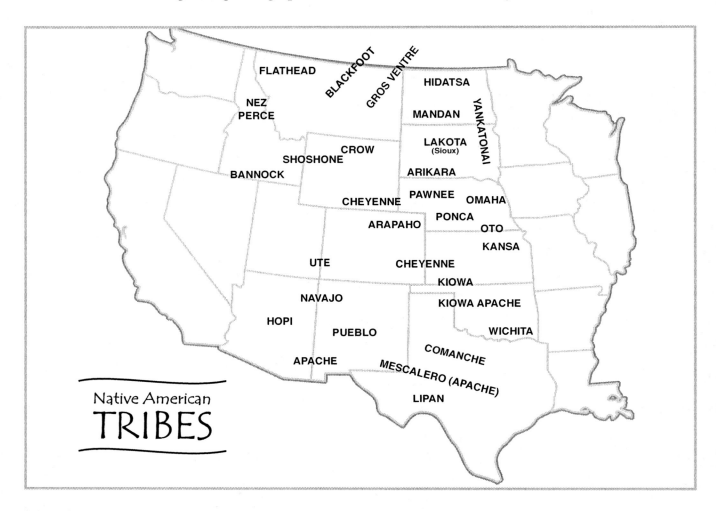

Directions: Listed below are states that became part of the United States as the country expanded westward. Using the map above and a current U.S. map, write down one Native American tribe that lived in each of these states.

1. Arizona _____

2. Colorado _____

3. Idaho _____

4. Kansas _____

5. Montana _____

6. Nebraska _____

7. New Mexico _____

8. North Dakota _____

9. Oklahoma _____

10. South Dakota _____

11. Texas _____

12. Wyoming _____

U.S. Expansion Map

The map below shows the land acquisitions of the United States and the years in which territories were acquired.

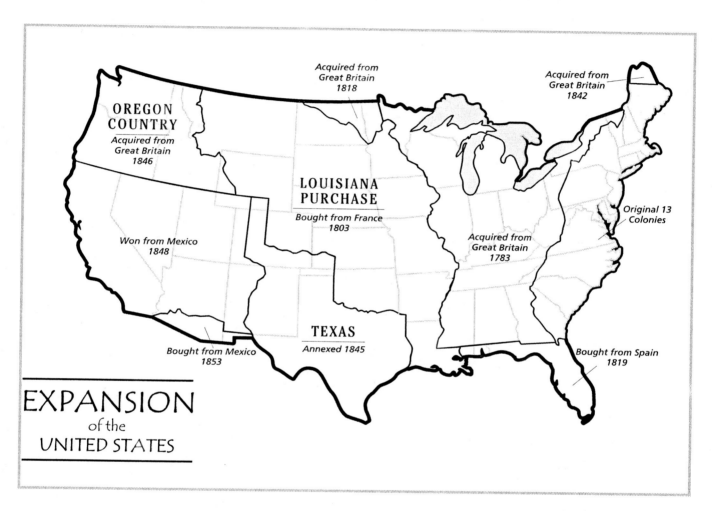

Directions: Use the map above and a current U.S. map to answer the following questions.

1. What seven U.S. states were partially or entirely created from land acquired by a treaty with Mexico in 1848? _____

2. Which three states were formed entirely from the Oregon Country? _____

3. What 14 states were formed in whole or in part from the Louisiana Purchase? _____

_____

4. Which three states were formed in whole or in part from land acquired from Spain in 1819?

_____

Frontier Railroads Map

The first transcontinental railroad was the Central Pacific and the Union Pacific. Later railroads were the Great Northern, the Atchison, Topeka, Santa Fe, and the Texas and Pacific (which connected New Orleans and Los Angeles).

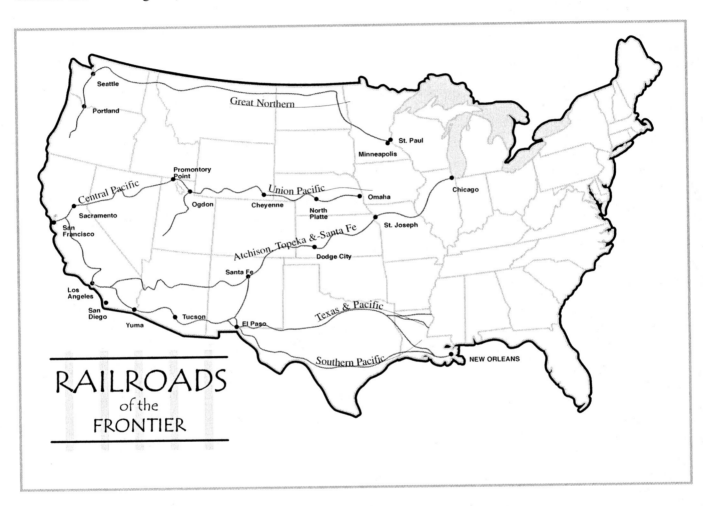

Directions: Use the above map and a current U.S. map to answer the following questions.

1. Name five states the Central Pacific and Union Pacific passed through. _____

2. List seven cities on the Central Pacific/Union Pacific route. _____

3. Name five states the Southern Pacific passed through. _____

4. List five cities on the Southern Pacific route. _____

5. Name six states along the Great Northern route. _____

6. Name seven states through which the Atchison, Topeka, & Santa Fe traveled. _____

7. Give three states that the Texas & Pacific went through. _____

Who Am I?

Directions: Match each of these famous Westerners with the correct description listed below. Refer to page 78 as needed.

Westerners

_____ 1. Brigham Young

_____ 2. Chief Joseph

_____ 3. Davy Crockett

_____ 4. Fanny Kelly

_____ 5. George Custer

_____ 6. George Donner

_____ 7. James Marshall

_____ 8. Jesse Chisholm

_____ 9. Jim Beckwourth

_____ 10. John Colter

_____ 11. Kit Carson

_____ 12. Laura Ingalls Wilder

_____ 13. Helen Hunt Jackson

_____ 14. Narcissa Whitman

_____ 15. Sam Houston

Descriptions

a. the first white man to explore the Yellowstone area

b. wrote about the mistreatment of Indians

c. led Mormons across the Great Plains to settle near the Great Salt Lake

d. black mountain man who lived with the Crow Indians for many years

e. guide and Indian agent

f. wrote a book about her captivity by Sioux Indians

g. led a group that got trapped in the mountains during winter

h. wrote a series of books for children about her life as a pioneer girl

i. a trader who followed a trail later used to drive cattle from Texas to Kansas

j. a hunter, Indian fighter, Congressman, and fighter at the Alamo

k. the leader of the Nez Perce who vowed to "fight no more forever"

l. a Civil War hero defeated by the Plains Indians at Little Big Horn

m. the leader of the Texas revolution against Mexico

n. a white missionary woman in the Oregon Territory

o. found gold at Sutter's Mill

Researching Frontier States

Directions: Choose a western state, or pick any state west of the original 13 states since each one was at some time a frontier state. Research the early history of the state looking for the following facts. Then use the tips at the bottom of the page to help you write a report about that state.

Frontier History

- Year settlers first moved into the territory
- Why early pioneers came to the state
- Problems early pioneers faced there
- First leaders in the territory or state
- Nation the U.S. got the territory from
- Year it became a U.S. territory
- Year it became a state

- Important frontier businesses
- Important early towns and cities
- First capital city
- Special advantages the state had
- Important rivers and trails
- Mountains and other physical features
- Natural resources

The State Today

- Current population
- Area in square miles
- Capital city

- Major cities
- Important products and businesses
- Special places to visit

Writing a Report

When writing a report, it is important to do the following:

- Use as many sources as possible, including textbooks, encyclopedias, Internet web sites, and books.

- Take notes carefully. Get all of the facts, but do not use complete sentences. Be sure to write down where you found the information, however, so you can refer back to it if needed or include the reference on the works-cited or bibliography page.

- Organize the notes by time and place, and use them to help write the report.

- When writing the report, use your own words. Do not copy sentences word-for-word from your notes. This is called *plagiarism* which means "stealing and passing off someone else's work as your own without giving credit to that person."

- Check spelling, especially of unfamiliar names and places.

- Carefully check your report for correct grammar, punctuation, margins, and other writing conventions.

- Neatly write or type the final copy of the report in paragraph format.

Researching Native American Tribes

Directions: Select one of the Native American tribes listed below (or another) to research. Use a variety of sources such as books, encyclopedias, and the Internet to answer the questions at the bottom of the page. Refer to the Writing a Report section on page 74 to help you write the report.

Native American Tribes

Algonquin	Cherokee	Hopi	Nez Perce
Apache	Cheyenne	Iroquois	Pawnee
Arapaho	Comanche	Kiowa	Shoshone
Arikara	Creek	Mandan	Sioux
Blackfoot	Crow	Navajo	Ute

Native American Questionnaire

Lifestyle

What is the name of the tribe?

In what present-day states did they live?

Where did they live (plains, woodlands, mountains, etc.)?

Did they live in permanent villages or were they nomadic?

Who were their important tribal leaders?

How were their leaders chosen?

What language did they speak?

What animals were important to the tribe?

At what age did young people marry?

What myths, legends, and religious beliefs did they have?

What jobs did men, women, boys, girls have?

Clothing

What garments were worn by women and girls? By men and boys?

What materials were used for clothing?

What hair styles were worn by adults and children?

Homes

What type of homes did they live in (tipi, wickiup, etc.)?

What materials were used to make their homes?

Were the homes permanent or easily moved?

How many people lived in a home (a single family, several families, or all the relatives of one family)?

Food

What was the basic food(s) of the tribe?

Did the tribe grow crops or harvest any wild foods?

What animals did the men hunt?

War

What weapons did they use for war?

Who were the traditional enemies of the tribe?

What battles did the tribe fight with settlers or the U.S. Army?

On what reservations were they forced to live?

Become a Famous Westerner

A great way to understand the Westward movement is to learn about and then "become" a famous person who lived during that time period. You not only become familiar with the person but also the times in which he or she lived.

Do the Research

Choose a pioneer, explorer, mountain man, Native American, cowboy, gold miner, adventurer, or other Westerner from the list on page 78. Use encyclopedias, biographies, the Internet, and other sources to find information about this person. Use the outline on page 77 to help guide your research.

Take notes, and write down the main facts about the person you chose. Find out the important dates, adventures, accomplishments, and failures of your character as well as interesting stories or events. Remember that you do not have to include every little detail about his or her life.

Organize your notes, and decide what things you want to include in your presentation. Use 3"x5" cards to write the main details and make an outline of what you want to say.

Practice giving your presentation out loud as if you were that person. Try to assume his or her attitude and personality. Refer to your note cards as needed, but do not just read your notes. Try giving your presentation in front of family members or a friend and get their input. Keep practicing until you feel comfortable.

Get in Costume

Put together an appropriate costume. Check your closets for pants, shirts, or old costumes which might work, or borrow articles of clothing from family members or friends. Hats can even be made from construction paper.

Use a Prop

Use a prop that fits with your character. It could be a book, metal pan for mining, tool, or similar item. (Make sure the prop is permitted at school.)

Stay in Character

Remember who you are portraying. Be serious, and avoid any silly behavior (unless your character was that way).

Be Dramatic

Speak clearly and loudly enough for the class to hear. Do not get nervous and rush through your presentation. Use your hands, arms, and prop to emphasize important points. Use facial and body gestures, and stride across the front of the room if appropriate. Have confidence in yourself.

Be Famous

One way to begin your presentation is to state, "My name is . . . ." Then continue by telling about your life, starting with your youth and moving on to your Western adventures. Tell about an interesting event or adventure. Most of all, have fun stepping back in time and becoming a famous Westerner!

Become a Famous Westerner *(cont.)*

Directions: Choose a famous Westerner from the list on page 78. Learn about that person and then give an oral report as if you are that person. Use the outline below to help you research important information about that Westerner. Note that you do not have to include all of the following details in your presentation.

Biographical Outline

I. Youth

   A. Birth place and date

   B. Home life and experiences

      1. Parents

      2. Brothers and sisters

      3. Places lived (parts of the country, farm or town)

      4. Circumstances (rich or poor, important events)

   C. Schooling (when, how much)

II. Western Adventures

   A. Frontier experiences

      1. Adventures and travels in the West

      2. Dangers faced (give details)

      3. Friends/companions

   B. Reasons for fame

      1. Accomplishments (describe)

      2. Leadership experiences

      3. Greatest challenges faced (give details)

   C. Interesting facts and stories

III. End of Life

   A. Death

      1. Date and place

      2. Age at death

      3. Facts about death

Famous Westerners

Andrew Jackson—first frontier president

Annie Oakley—sharpshooter in Wild West shows

Betty Zane—heroine of Fort Henry

Brigham Young—leader of the Mormon migration west

Buffalo Bill Cody—had a Wild West show

Catherine Sagar—pioneer girl orphaned on the way West

Charles Goodnight—legendary cattleman

Charles Russell—artist who painted cowboys and Indians

Charlie Siringo—first cowboy author

Chief Joseph—Nez Perce chief

Crazy Horse—Sioux leader who defeated Custer

Davy Crockett—legendary frontiersman

Fanny Kelly—wrote a book about her captivity by Sioux Indians

Frederic Remington—Western artist

George Catlin—artist who wanted to save Indians and the wilderness

George Custer—Army general killed at Little Big Horn

George Donner—led a group of settlers that got trapped in the mountains in winter

Geronimo—Apache leader

Helen Hunt Jackson—wrote of the mistreatment of Indians

Hugh Glass—tough mountain man

James Marshall—discovered gold at Sutter's Mill in California

James Polk—U.S. president who wanted Oregon and Spanish lands

Jedediah Smith—explored the West farther than any man

Jesse Chisholm—trader who marked the trail named for him

Jim Beckwourth—trapper and Crow Indian leader

Jim Bowie—fought and died at the Alamo

Jim Bridger—explorer and Army scout

Joe Meek—trapper and explorer

John C. Fremont—explored much of the far West

John Chapman ("Johnny Appleseed")—spent his life planting apple trees

John Colter—explored Yellowstone area

John Wesley Powell—explorer of the Grand Canyon

Kit Carson—guide and Indian agent

Laura Ingalls Wilder—wrote the story of her pioneer experiences

Manuel Lisa—ran a fur trapping and trading business

Mark Twain (Samuel Clemens)—author and newspaper writer

Meriwether Lewis—co-leader of Lewis and Clark Expedition

Narcissa Whitman—missionary and one of the first pioneer women in Oregon

Nat Love—black cowboy and author

Robert Stuart—helped lay out the route of the Oregon Trail

Sacagawea—guide and translator on the Lewis and Clark Expedition

Sam Houston—frontiersman who led the fight for Texas independence

Sarah Winnemucca—first Indian woman to write a book

Sitting Bull—Sioux chief who defeated Custer

Tecumseh—Shawnee chief who wanted Indians to unite and fight

Theodore Roosevelt—U.S. president, ex-cowboy, and outdoorsman

Virginia Reed—Donner Party survivor

Wild Bill Hickok—soldier, gambler, lawman, gunfighter

William Clark—co-leader of Lewis and Clark Expedition

Wyatt Earp—lawman and gunman

Teacher Lesson Plans for Art and Music

Western Art and Music

Objective: Students will further their understanding of the Western era by replicating homes, crafts, and artifacts related to pioneer life and Native Americans.

Materials: copies of Your Own Covered Wagon (page 80); copies of Cattle Brands (page 81); copies of Pioneer Homes (page 82); copies of Great Plains Indian Beadwork (pages 83–85); materials listed on each page; pictures of pioneer homes and artifacts for reference

Procedure

1. Collect the materials listed on each page before assigning a project.

2. Reproduce and distribute copies of Your Own Covered Wagon (page 80). Review the project, distribute materials, and instruct students to follow the directions for making a model of a covered wagon. If desired, allow students to work with a partner.

3. Reproduce and distribute the Cattle Brands (page 81) activity sheet. Introduce the activity, and have students complete the assignment independently. As an extension, students can design their own cattle brand.

4. Reproduce and distribute copies of Pioneer Homes (page 82). Review the project, distribute materials, and tell students to read the directions for making models of a log cabin and sod house. Explain that the roof will be able to be lifted off so that the house's interior will show.

5. Reproduce and distribute copies of Great Plains Indian Beadwork (pages 83–85). Read and discuss the background information on page 83. Be sure all materials are available beforehand. Students should use the model illustration to assemble the loom. Adult assistance may be necessary, and supervision is required for the loom assembly. Students may work in pairs or individually for this project. When beadwork projects are completed, encourage students to display them. Have students discuss their experiences as they built the loom and wove their creations.

Assessment: Assess students' completion of each project and ability to follow directions instead of students' artistic ability.

Your Own Covered Wagon

Pioneers traveled West in covered wagons which were incredibly durable, often able to float, and capable of carrying several thousand pounds of furniture, tools, clothing, and personal belongings.

Making a Covered Wagon

Materials: a small box (open on one side); brown paint or paper; brown construction paper or tagboard; white construction paper or copy paper; butcher paper; gray and dark-colored construction paper; craft sticks; tape; glue; markers; cloth; toothpicks or straws; scissors

Procedure

1. Use a small box as the base of your covered wagon. Cover it with brown paper, or paint it brown.

2. Make the driver's seat, tool box, water keg, and animal feed box on the wagon from brown construction paper or tagboard. Use a craft stick for the brake lever.

3. Make a cover for the wagon out of white construction or copy paper. Tape it in place on the inside of the box.

4. Cut wheels out of cardboard or tagboard and glue them onto the wagon.

5. Use small pieces of construction paper, tagboard, cloth, or butcher paper to make the tools, clothing, and equipment to display in or near the wagon. Refer to the list below of items that pioneers often carried in their wagons. Toothpicks or straws can be used for tool handles.

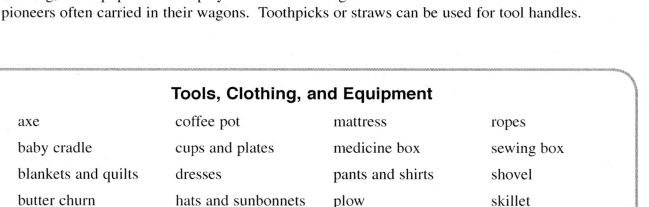

Tools, Clothing, and Equipment

axe	coffee pot	mattress	ropes
baby cradle	cups and plates	medicine box	sewing box
blankets and quilts	dresses	pants and shirts	shovel
butter churn	hats and sunbonnets	plow	skillet
camp stool	lantern	rifle	washtub

Cattle Brands

Cowboys branded the symbol of their ranch into the hides of their cattle and horses so that everyone could tell whose animals they were. They used a hot, metal branding iron, which burned away the hair on the animal's hide and permanently imprinted the brand.

Directions: Pictured below are the brands for several ranches. Under each brand, write the name that it matches. The names are as follows.

Bar 9	Diamond Bar	Flying V	Rocking Horse
Box L	Double 6	Lazy J	Rocking R
Circle T	Double Bar X	Rising Sun	Triple D

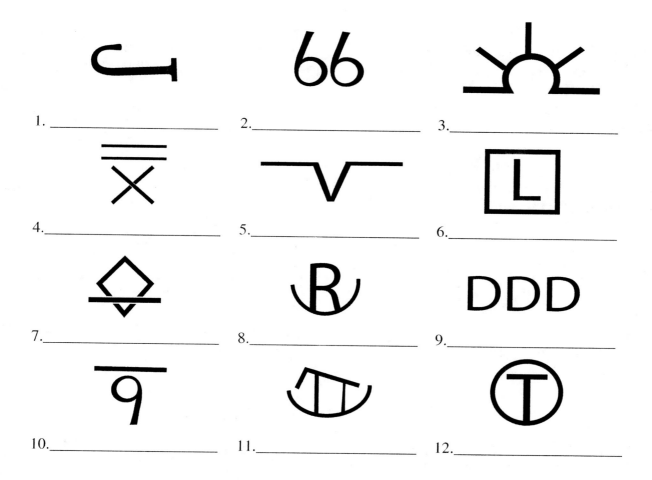

1. _____

2. _____

3. _____

4. _____

5. _____

6. _____

7. _____

8. _____

9. _____

10. _____

11. _____

12. _____

Extension

On a separate sheet of paper, design your own brand. Include the meaning or significance of the symbol.

Pioneer Homes

Pioneers lived in different types of houses, depending on what materials were available. Create a model of a log cabin or sod house using the materials listed below. Also make clothing, furniture, tools, and other things that pioneers had. Find pictures in books or on the Internet to make your model pioneer home and items as historically accurate as possible.

Building a Log Cabin

Materials: a sturdy piece of cardboard for the base; drinking straws, craft sticks, dowels, or small sticks; glue or masking tape; brown tempera paint; modeling or sculpting clay; small rocks; construction paper or tagboard; toothpicks; small pieces of cloth; colored markers; cardboard (for the roof)

Procedure

1. Assemble the cabin on a sturdy piece of cardboard which will serve as the base.

2. Use drinking straws, craft sticks, dowels, or small sticks to make the cabin walls. Glue or tape these in place, and then connect the four walls together. Remember to include a door and windows. If needed, paint the cabin with brown tempera to look like logs.

3. Make the fireplace with clay and then stick small rocks into the clay, or use a marker to draw a fireplace on construction paper or tagboard.

4. Make the furniture, tools, cookware, clothing, and other items out of construction paper, tagboard, toothpicks, cloth, or other materials. Use markers to decorate the items, and place them in the cabin.

5. Design the roof so that it can be lifted off to see the inside of the cabin. To do so, take a piece of cardboard or tagboard and cover it with craft sticks or straws.

Building a Sod House

Materials: a sturdy piece of cardboard for the base; modeling or sculpting clay; craft sticks; construction paper or tagboard; toothpicks; small pieces of cloth; colored markers; cardboard; plant stems

Procedure

1. Build the cabin on a sturdy piece of cardboard which will serve as the base.

2. Use strips of clay to make the cabin walls and craft sticks to help reinforce the walls. As an alternative, use brown construction paper and use markers to draw blocks of sod on the walls.

3. Use clay to make the fireplace, or draw a fireplace on construction paper or tagboard.

4. Make the furniture, tools, cookware, clothing, and other items out of construction paper, tagboard, toothpicks, cloth, or other materials. Then put them in the sod house.

5. Use a piece of cardboard for the roof, covering it with clay and plant stems so that it can be lifted off to see the inside of the sod house.

Great Plains Indian Beadwork

The natives of the Great Plains were master artists and craftsmen who loved to decorate almost everything they used or wore. Many exquisite examples of the clothing, moccasins, and utility containers such as parfleches, tobacco and pipe cases, and quivers may be seen in museums featuring Native American exhibits.

Before the white man came to North America, designs were done in materials which were native to the continent. Nothing was wasted. Shells, porcupine quills, natural paints, and even elk teeth were used. The designs used by a tribe were passed down by family members, and the clothing thus trimmed was highly prized. Designs were traditional, and many of them were symbolic. For example, a cross symbolized four winds, and a zigzag line symbolized lightning. Wampum was made from shells which were shaped and polished. Some typical designs are given below.

After the coming of the white man, French traders brought glass beads made in Italy to trade for furs. The large ones called *pony beads* were soon used to make decorations formerly made with porcupine quills. After about 1850, however, *seed beads* from Czechoslovakia became the favorites.

Originally, the thread used for stringing came from sinew, the tough, fibrous, connective tissue of animals. This would be split into strands fine enough to thread through the beads. When cotton thread became available, however, it soon took the place of sinew. Today, nylon thread may also be used, and crochet thread no. 30 is a good choice for loom threads. (Waxing the threads prevents tangling.)

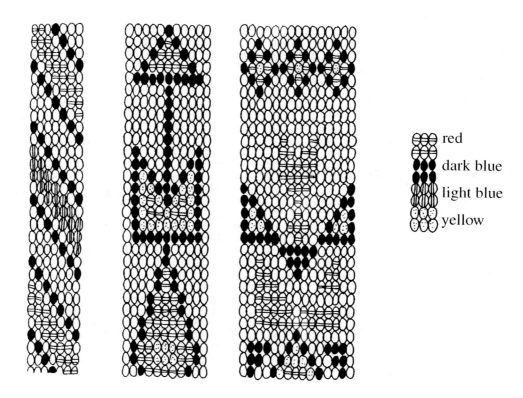

red
dark blue
light blue
yellow

Activity

Make your own design on graph paper. Use fine-tipped markers or colored pencils.

Great Plains Indian Beadwork *(cont.)*

Making the Loom

Materials: 1 piece white pine or similar wood 1/2" (1.25 cm) thick; 2 pieces white pine 4" x 6" x 1/2" (10 cm x 15 cm x 1.25 cm); ten 1" (2.5 cm) screws; 1 curtain spring about 3/8" (1 cm) in diameter (found in variety or hardware stores); 2 small, large-headed carpet tacks

Procedure

Assemble as illustrated.

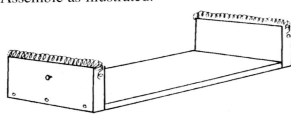
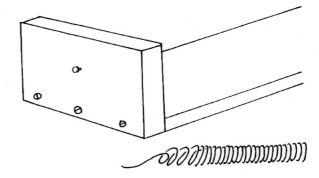

Beadwork Headband

Materials: beads in various colors; thread (no. 40); one package fine bead needles; one piece beeswax or a candle stub; graph paper (small size) for planning designs; colored crayons or pencils

Procedure

1. Tie the thread to the carpet tack at one end.

2. String the thread through the spring and around the carpet tack at the other end. Continue wrapping thread in this way until the width of the rows of thread is the one you wish for your headband.

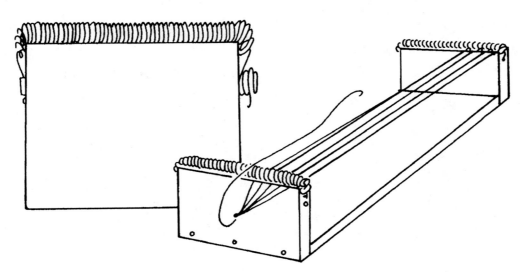

Great Plains Indian Beadwork *(cont.)*

Beadwork Headband *(cont.)*

3. Now that the loom is threaded, the fun begins. Be patient with the first row. It sometimes takes a little effort to get it straight. Once it is complete, however, the rest is easy.

4. Draw a design on graph paper, with one square standing for each bead, and use crayons or pencils to mark the colors.

5. Thread the needle with a long thread. Double it and tie the ends in a knot. Wax the knot and tie it to the outer loom thread nearest you.

6. Pick up the beads needed for the first row, according to your design plan, and thread them on the needle, sliding the beads down to the loom strings. Pass the needle under the loom strings, and with your left index finger move the beads into position with one bead between each pair of strings.

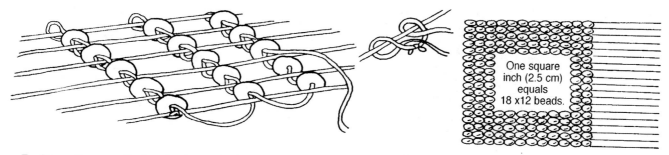

One square inch (2.5 cm) equals 18 x 12 beads.

7. Pass the needle back through the loom strings on the opposite side of the first thread. Pull the thread so the beads fit tightly.

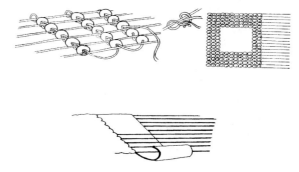

8. Repeat the weaving row by row, following your paper design. When you need to change to a new thread, start your weaving by passing the needle and thread through five or six beads of the last row and then continue. To end a thread without knotting, pass the needle once around the outer loom string and then through four or five beads before cutting.

9. When the beadwork is complete, finish off the ends by placing a piece of gummed paper tape below the loom strings. Cut the loom strings along this tape.

Teacher Lesson Plans for Science and Math

The Science of Gold Panning

Objectives: Students will conduct experiments to understand how sediment of different weights separates in water and how this helped miners pan for gold.

Materials: copies of Panning for Gold (page 87) and materials listed on page 87 including: sturdy metal pan or pie pan; a cup; dirt, sand, gravel, small rocks; water; timer or watch; a plastic jar with lid

Procedure

1. Before beginning the project, collect the materials needed.

2. Reproduce and distribute copies of Panning for Gold. Distribute the materials, read the directions in the Panning section, and demonstrate how to use the pan to sift out the heavier materials.

3. Next, make the sediment jar as described in the text. Have students observe the changes in the sediment lines as instructed and write the results on the Sediment Observation Record at the bottom of the page.

Assessment: Have students share their results with the class and discuss their results.

Math on the Western Trails

Objectives: Students will apply math skills to calculate distances and the number of people who traveled West.

Materials: copies of Western Trail Facts and Figures (page 88); copies of Gold Rush Prices (page 89); calculators (optional)

Procedure

1. Reproduce and distribute the Western Trail Facts and Figures activity sheet. Review the assignment and the math processes involved. Have students answer the questions independently.

2. Reproduce and distribute the Gold Rush Prices activity sheet. Have students complete the aasignment independently.

Assessment: Correct the activity sheets together.

Panning for Gold

The Forty-Niners used pans and water to separate the heavier gold from the lighter dirt, sand, rocks, and minerals. Try the experiments below to find the heaviest material.

Panning

Materials: sturdy metal pan or pie pan; a cup; dirt, sand, gravel, small rocks; water; timer or watch

Procedure

NOTE: Do this project outside as it can be messy.

1. Mix together a cup of dirt, sand, gravel, and small rocks in the pan.
2. Add 3 cups of water.
3. Use both hands to firmly hold the edge of the pan, and gently swirl the pan for two minutes.
4. Gradually splash out the water, dirt, and sand.
5. Examine the materials that are left in the pan. Compare them to what was splashed out. Are they heavier or lighter?

Sediment Jars

Materials: plastic jar with lid; water; a cup; dirt, sand, gravel, small rocks; timer or watch

Procedure

1. Fill the jar two-thirds full of water.
2. Pour a cup of dirt, sand, gravel, and small rocks into the jar of water. Put the lid on the jar.
3. Shake the jar for two minutes until everything is stirred up.
4. Place the jar where it will not be disturbed.
5. Watch what happens in the next 15 minutes.
6. Record your findings in the Sediment Observation Record below.
7. Then observe and record what happens one hour later, the next day, and the next week.

Sediment Observation Record

15 minutes later: _____

1 hour later: _____

Next day: _____

Next week: _____

Western Trail Facts and Figures

Directions: Use your math skills to solve the following problems about travel along the Western trails.

1. The Oregon Trail was 2,170 miles long. One branch of the Santa Fe Trail was 900 miles long. How much longer was the Oregon Trail?

2. In 1842, 125 pioneers followed the Oregon Trail. The following year 875 people used the trail, and then the next year 1,475 pioneers took this route. In 1845, 2,500 settlers traveled along this trail. What was the total number of people who went on the Oregon Trail during those four years?

3. In 1849, only 450 people traveled to Oregon along the Oregon Trail, but 25,500 took the California Trail to the gold fields. How many more people went to California?

4. Forty-Niners could take the ocean voyage around South America to California which was 13,000 miles long, or they could take the Oregon-California Trail which was 2,200 miles long. How many more miles was the ocean voyage?

5. One branch of the Santa Fe Trail was 780 miles long. The Cimarron Crossing was 100 miles shorter but more dangerous. How long was the Cimarron route?

6. Fort Laramie was 650 miles west of Independence, Missouri, where the Oregon Trail began. How many more miles did pioneers have to go before their 2,170-mile journey was over?

7. Independence Rock was 900 miles from Independence, Missouri. How far was it from the end of their 2,170-mile journey?

8. Fort Hall in Idaho was 1,200 miles from Independence, Missouri. How many more miles did the pioneers have to travel to reach Oregon, a 2,170-mile trip from Independence?

9. The transcontinental railroad was 1,775 miles long and reached from Omaha, Nebraska, to Sacramento, California. The Central Pacific laid 690 miles of track. The rest was built by the Union Pacific Railroad. How many miles did they build?

10. The bed of a covered wagon was 6 feet wide, 12 feet long, and 3 feet high. What was the volume of the wagon bed?

Gold Rush Prices

The prices that gold miners had to pay for goods varied during the gold rush, depending on where they were. Regardless of location, however, the prices were high. Look at the prices listed below for an idea of what things cost back then.

Prices at an 1848 Mining Camp

Food		Clothing and Supplies	
beans (1 pound)	$10.00	overalls	$45.00
bread (1 loaf)	$2.00	pair of boots	$100.00
can of sardines	$16.00	pan (for gold)	$15.00
coffee (1 pound)	$40.00	pickax	$50.00
dozen eggs	$3.00	shirt	$20.00
sausage (1 pound)	$5.00		

Directions: Use the above prices to solve the following word problems.

1. How much would it cost to buy five pounds of beans and one pound of coffee? _____

2. How much would a pair of overalls, a shirt, and a pair of boots cost? _____

3. Sam Garcia bought a pan, a pickax, three pounds of beans, bread, a can of sardines, and a dozen eggs. How much did he spend in all? _____

4. Jeremiah Smith found $20 worth of gold. He bought a pound of sausage, a dozen eggs, and a loaf of bread. How much did he have left? _____

5. The Johnson brothers bought a can of sardines, half a pound of coffee, bread, 10 pounds of beans, two pans, and a pickax. How much did they spend altogether? _____

6. Jonas Atkins wore out his boots and needs to buy a new pair. If he typically makes $5.00 per day panning for gold, how many days will it be before he can buy the boots? _____

7. Wong Lee made $500 doing laundry for miners. If he spent 30 percent of that on food and supplies, how much did he have left? _____

8. Old Tom Jenkins made $200 on his claim. He lost one-fourth of it by gambling. Then he bought a new shirt and pair of overalls. How much did he have left? _____

9. Four miners split the cost of two cans of sardines, three pounds of sausage, a pound of coffee, two loaves of bread, a dozen eggs, a pickax, and 20 pounds of beans. How much did each miner have to pay? _____

10. Alfonso Rinalti mined $250 worth of gold at his claim. What food, clothing, and supplies could he purchase with that amount of money? _____

Culminating Activities

Pioneer Day

Set aside one day to devote to activities related to your study of the westward movement in the United States. You could call it Pioneer Day, Western Day, or Frontier Day.

Parent Help

Encourage parents or adult family members to help set up, monitor, and enjoy the activities. See if they have any special talents, interests, or hobbies that would be a match for specific centers.

Costumes

Encourage students to come in western, Native American, or pioneer attire and to wear leather shoes, boots, or moccasins instead of tennis shoes. Books about western life and Internet web sites offer many illustrations. Ask one or two adult helpers to use makeup to add some mustaches and beards and give boys a period look for the day.

Eat Hearty

Plan a luncheon with a western theme. Bread and soup or stew were simple foods that most pioneers ate. Have students make table decorations at one of the centers. Make sure students do not have any food allergies or dietary restrictions.

Centers

The centers you set up should relate in some way to the western period or activities from this book. Centers should allow small groups of six or seven students to participate. Each center should take about 20 minutes. Students should then rotate to the next activity. The following are suggestions for various centers. Add others for which you have special expertise.

☐ **Create a Wagon Train**

Use small boxes, straws, craft sticks, and other materials to construct covered wagons as described on page 80. By the end of the day, the class will have an entire wagon train.

☐ **Pioneer Homes**

Students at this center can build pioneer homes, barns, and farms using construction paper, craft sticks, fabric pieces, small sticks, and other materials. Provide books or pictures of various frontier homes. The activities on page 82 can be done here.

☐ **Indian Tipis and Villages**

At this center, students can make tipis as described on page 83 or other tribal homes such as wickiups or lodges. Provide pictures of these as well as materials such as craft sticks, straws, felt, and construction paper.

Culminating Activities *(cont.)*

Centers *(cont.)*

☐ **Trading Posts and Forts**

A western Army fort or trading post can be constructed by students working at this center. Provide craft sticks, straws, and other materials. Have pictures for reference.

☐ **Frontier Games**

At this center, students can play games that frontier children enjoyed like foot races, hide and seek, tag, and snap the whip. (In snap the whip, children form a line while holding hands and then try to "snap" off the last child in the line by moving quickly together.)

☐ **Music Center**

Have recordings of some of the favorite songs of the period, or teach students some of these songs. Use the Laura Ingalls Wilder Songbook or search the Internet for copies of songs such as "Sweet Betsy from Pike," "Old Dan Tucker," and "Clementine."

☐ **Dance**

Learn and practice a simple square dance, or have students create their own dances to music that pioneers or cowboys would have listened to.

☐ **Pioneer Crafts and Skills**

Have students try their hand at pioneer crafts: churning butter, using a simple hand loom, sewing, knitting or crocheting, knot tying, or making soap or candles.

☐ **Indian Shields, Drums, and Masks**

Students at this center can make an Indian shield (see page 84) or a tom-tom (page 85). Native American masks can also be recreated at this center using the papier-mâché techniques described on page 84 for making the shields.

☐ **Readers' Theater**

Students can practice the Hugh Glass readers' theater script on pages 60–62 to present to the class or write their own script based on a famous western character or event.

☐ **Model Boats**

Provide craft sticks and straws for students to build models of rafts, keelboats, and ferry boats that were used to carry covered wagons and people across rivers. For steamboats and paddleboats, use Styrofoam trays for the hull and craft sticks, pipe cleaners, and additional materials for the other parts. Provide pictures for students to use for reference.

☐ **Clay Figures or Busts**

Students can use modeling or sculpting clay to sculpt westerners, horses, wagons, or other things they have learned about. A 25-pound bag of clay can be sliced into 18 or more rectangular blocks of clay with a piece of fishing line. Use toothpicks or plastic utensils to carve the features. Have paper towels available for clean up.

Annotated Bibliography

Nonfiction

Alter, Judith. *Women of the Old West*. Franklin Watts, 1989. (Good account of some remarkable western women)

Blackwood, Gary L. *Life on the Oregon Trail*. Lucent, 1999. (Detailed, interesting account of life on the trail)

Duncan, Dayton. *The West: An Illustrated History for Children*. Little, Brown, 1996. (Based on PBS/Ken Burns television series, very informative)

Freedman, Russell. *In the Days of the Vaqueros: America's First True Cowboys*. Clarion, 2001. (Detailed and colorful account of cowboys)

Glass, Andrew. *Mountain Men: True Grit and Tall Tales*. Doubleday, 2001. (Amusing, colorful accounts of individual mountain men)

Hicks, Peter. *You Wouldn't Want to Live in a Wild West Town!* Franklin Watts, 2004. (Humorous take on life in a western town)

Josephson, Judith Pinkerton. *Growing Up in Pioneer America*. Lerner, 2003. (Excellent writing, interesting quotes, and good details about pioneer life)

Kallen, Stuart A. *Life on the American Frontier*. Lucent, 1999. (Superior, detailed accounts of westward movement with primary sources)

Kalman, Bobbie. *Bandannas, Chaps, and Ten-Gallon Hats*. Crabtree, 1999. (Great information on cowboy dress)

———. *The Wagon Train*. Crabtree, 1999. (Good information in simple format and language)

———. *Women of the West*. Crabtree, 2000. (Interesting vignettes of women's lives)

Lavender, David. *The Santa Fe Trail*. Holiday House, 1995. (Solid history of the trail)

Morley, Jacqueline. *You Wouldn't Want to Be an American Pioneer!* Franklin Watts, 2002. (Humorous take on the pioneer life)

Ritchie, David. *Frontier Life*. (Excellent overview of life on the frontier)

Sanford, William R. *The Chisholm Trail in American History*. Enslow, 2000. (Good overview of the trail and cowboy life)

Sherrow, Victoria. *Life During the Gold Rush*. Lucent, 1998. (Detailed account of the gold rush)

Stefoff, Rebecca. *Children of the Westward Trail*. Millbrook, 1996. (Outstanding, detailed account of life for pioneer children)

———. *The Opening of the West*. Cavendish, 2003. (Exceptional accounts with primary sources of the opening of the West)

Sundling, Charles W. *Mountain Men of the Frontier*. ABDO, 2000. (Interesting stories of the mountain men).

———. *Native Americans of the Frontier*. ABDO, 2000. (Brief treatment of life for Native Americans in contact with pioneers)

———. *Women of the Frontier*. ABDO, 2000. (Good account of women's daily lives on the frontier)

Teacher Created Resources Products

A Guide for Using Little House in the Big Woods in the Classroom. TCR0522.

A Guide for Using Little House on the Prairie in the Classroom. TCR0539.

Westward Expansion Multimedia Collection CD. TCR3041.

Westward Ho Thematic Unit. TCR0282.

Glossary

bandana—handkerchief tied around a cowboy's neck

barter—to trade food or goods for needed supplies

bee—a group of pioneers making a quilt, raising a barn, or working together in some way

bonnet—pioneer girl's hat that is tied under her chin

brand—a mark of ownership burned into an animal's hide

buckskin—leather clothes made from deerskin

chaps—leather leggings worn over pants by cowboys

cholera—a deadly, contagious disease spread by unclean water

claim—to say that an area of land belongs to you

contagious—diseases easily spread by human contact

Dutch oven—a covered iron pot used to cook food by placing hot coals under and over it

emigrants—people who leave a country or region to settle in another place

fiddle—a violin

ford—to cross a river

Great Plains—the land from the Mississippi River to the Rocky Mountains from Canada to South Texas

homestead—government land granted to farm families

immigrants—people who come into a country to live

jerky—meat that is dried over a fire to preserve it

lode—a vein of gold or silver in a rock crack

massacre—the deliberate, merciless killing of many people

mill—a building with machines for making products

nomads—people who have no permanent home

pass—a route through mountains

pelt—animal skin

pioneer—a person who leads the way in settling a new land

placer—sand or dirt with gold in a stream

population—the number of people in an area

prairie schooner—a covered wagon

prospectors—miners looking for gold

reservations—land set aside by the government for Native Americans

rodeo—a show featuring cowboy skills

slough—place with soft, deep mud

sluices—man-made wooden water channels

stampede—a group of animals panicked into a wild run

steers—young, male cattle

suffrage—the right to vote

tipi (tepee)—tent home made of poles and animal hides

transcontinental—to span the continent from ocean to ocean

treaty—an agreement made between nations or peoples

Answer Key

Page 34
1. a
2. b
3. c
4. a
5. d
6. d
7. c
8. d
9. b
10. a

Page 35
1. c
2. b
3. c
4. b
5. d
6. a
7. b
8. d
9. a
10. c

Page 36
1. c
2. d
3. c
4. b
5. a
6. c
7. a
8. b
9. d
10. d

Page 37
1. b
2. a
3. c
4. d
5. d
6. c
7. d
8. b
9. c
10. b

Page 38
1. c
2. a
3. d
4. d
5. a
6. c
7. c
8. a
9. d
10. b

Page 39
1. b
2. d
3. b
4. d
5. b
6. b
7. c
8. a
9. c
10. d

Page 40
1. b
2. a
3. d
4. a
5. c
6. d
7. a
8. d
9. a
10. c

Page 41
1. a
2. d
3. c
4. d
5. a
6. b
7. c
8. a
9. c
10. b

Page 45
1. m
2. d
3. i
4. j
5. h
6. k
7. c
8. n
9. b
10. e
11. g
12. o
13. f
14. a
15. l

Answer Key *(cont.)*

Page 46

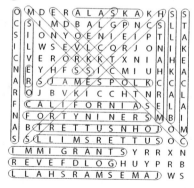

Page 47

Across

1. chaps
4. spurs
6. mustangs
8. branding iron
9. longhorns
10. corral
11. trail boss
13. bronco buster
15. stirrup
16. roundup
17. lasso
18. saddle

Down

1. chuck wagon
2. cattle rustler
3. bandana
5. wrangler
7. horses
12. stampede
13. bridle
14. beans

Page 55

Comprehension Questions-

1. the dogs
2. Sarah makes pets of the chickens.
3. She throws the hair to the birds.
4. colored pencils
5. yes
6. Their mother had sung to them.
7. "Sumer Is Icumen in" (Summer Is Coming)
8. to show the sea
9. to make a dune to slide on
10. Matthew and Maggie

Discussion Questions

(Answers may vary.)

1. Caleb; he missed his mother a great deal.
2. She is not pretty and is tall.
3. the sea
4. The cat stays in the house, not the barn.
5. Caleb asks daily about his mother. They miss her singing. They try to remember her ways.
6. Sarah wears men's overalls. She repairs the roof. She wants to drive Jack.
7. She gives hair to the birds. She pets the sheep. She adopts the chickens as pets. The dogs love her.
8. Yes, Sarah is kind and caring with both children. She teaches them to sing and draw. She talks about her past life.
9. No, Sarah liked stormy weather.
10. Answers will vary.

Page 67

1. South Dakota and Wyoming
2. Oregon and Washington
3. Montana, North Dakota, and South Dakota
4. Nebraska
5. Wyoming, Idaho, Oregon, and Washington
6. Wyoming
7. Arizona, California, Idaho, Iowa, Kansas, Missouri, Montana, Nebraska, Nevada, North Dakota, Oregon, South Dakota, Utah, Washington, Wyoming

Page 69

1. Oregon Trail, California Trail, Mormon Trail, Santa Fe Trail, Old Spanish Trail, and the Gila River Trail
2. Independence, Missouri
3. California and Oregon
4. Nauvoo, Illinois
5. Salt Lake City, Utah
6. Old Spanish Trail
7. Gila River Trail
8. Oregon Trail or Oregon-California Trail
9. Rocky Mountains and Sierra Nevada
10. Gila River Trail and Old Spanish Trail
11. California Trail
12. Oregon Trail
13. California Trail
14. Oregon Trail and Mormon Trail

Answer Key *(cont.)*

Page 70

1. *Arizona*–Hopi, Apache, and Navajo
2. *Colorado*–Arapaho, Cheyenne, and Ute
3. *Idaho*–Nez Perce, Bannock, and Shoshone
4. *Kansas*–Cheyenne, Kansa, Kiowa
5. *Montana*–Flathead, Blackfoot, Gros Ventre, and Nez Perce
6. *Nebraska*–Ponca, Omaha, Pawnee, and Oto
7. *New Mexico*–Apache, Mescaleno, Navajo, and Pueblo
8. *North Dakota*–Mandan, Hidatsa, and Yankatonai
9. *Oklahoma*–Kiowa Apache and Wichita
10. *South Dakota*–Lakota (Sioux), Arikara, and Yankatonai
11. *Texas*–Kiowa, Apache, Comanche, Mescalero (Apache), and Lipan
12. *Wyoming*–Cheyenne, Crow, and Shoshone

Page 71

1. Arizona, California, Colorado, Nevada, New Mexico, Utah, and Wyoming
2. Idaho, Oregon, and Washington
3. Arkansas, Colorado, Iowa, Kansas, Louisiana, Minnesota, Missouri, Montana, Nebraska, New Mexico, North Dakota, Oklahoma, South Dakota, and Wyoming
4. Alabama, Florida, and Mississippi

Page 72

1. California, Nebraska, Nevada, Utah, and Wyoming
2. Cheyenne, North Platte, Ogden, Omaha, Promontory Point, Sacramento, and San Francisco
3. Arizona, California, Louisiana, New Mexico, and Texas
4. El Paso, Los Angeles, New Orleans, Tucson, and Yuma
5. Idaho, Minnesota, Montana, North Dakota, Oregon, and Washington
6. Arizona, California, Colorado, Illinois, Kansas, Missouri, and New Mexico
7. Louisiana, Texas, and New Mexico

Page 73

1. c
2. k
3. j
4. f
5. l
6. g
7. o
8. i
9. d
10. a
11. e
12. h
13. b
14. n
15. m

Page 81

1. Lazy J
2. Double 6
3. Rising Sun
4. Double Bar X
5. Flying V
6. Box L
7. Diamond Bar
8. Rocking R
9. Triple D
10. Bar 9
11. Rocking Horse
12. Circle T

Page 88

1. 1,270 miles
2. 4,975 people
3. 25,050 people
4. 10,800 miles
5. 680 miles
6. 1,520 miles
7. 1,270 miles
8. 970 miles
9. 1,085 miles
10. 216 cubic feet

Page 89

1. $90
2. $165
3. $116
4. $10
5. $218
6. 20 days
7. $350
8. $85
9. $86
10. Answers will vary.